A Hundred Customs and Traditions of Tibetan People

by
Sagong Wangdu

Translated *by*
Tenzin Tsepak

LIBRARY OF TIBETAN WORKS AND ARCHIVES

Copyright © 2009: Library of Tibetan Works and Archives

First Print 2009
Reprint 2013

ALL RIGHTS RESERVED

No portion of this publication may be reproduced, stored in a retrieval system, or transmitted in any form or by any means, electronic, mechanical, photo-copying, recording or otherwise, without the prior permission of the bearers of copyright.

Illustrations by Namgyal Phuntsok

ISBN: 978-81-86470-96-1

Published by the Library of Tibetan Works and Archives, Dharamsala, and printed at Indraprastha Press (CBT), 4 Bahadur Shah Zafar Marg, New Delhi-110002

CONTENTS

	Publisher's Note	v
	Translator's Note	vii
1.	Offering Substances	1
2.	Customs and Traditions	11
3.	Tibetan Performing Arts	21
4.	Types of Design	29
5.	Architectural Designs	39
6.	Recreation	43
7.	Marriage Customs	47
8.	Bon and the Five Traditions of Tibetan Buddhism	53
9.	Festivals	61
10.	Things to Avoid	75
11.	Lifestyle	83
12.	Death Ceremonies and Funeral Rites	91
13.	Kinds of Decoration	95
14.	Other Customs	99

PUBLISHER'S NOTE

A Hundred Customs and Traditions of Tibetan People gives a clear overview of some of the unique customs and traditions of the Tibetan people. Originally written by Sagong Wangdu, this work has been carefully translated into English by Tenzin Tsepak. On the 50th anniversary of the Tibetan people's uprising and exodus into exile, The Library of Tibetan Works and Archives is delighted to publish this text. It aims to benefit Tibetan youth and English-speaking readers from around the world in further understanding various aspects of Tibetan customs and traditions.

We hope this publication will make its small contribution to the Library's continued efforts towards preservation, dissemination and continuation of the rich culture of Tibet which unfortunately is at the verge of extinction in Tibet itself.

Geshe Lhakdor
Director

19th August 2009

Translator's note

A Hundred Customs and Traditions of Tibetan People is a translation of a book compiled and written by Sagong Wangdu and published by the People's Publishing House in 2003. The book is intended to help foreigners and young Tibetan guides in negotiating the terrain of Tibetan culturalscape. The author claims the book to be free from his authorial judgments and an exact representation of the customs and traditions of Tibetan people as they exist in their lifestyle.

The English translation is made available with the dual purpose of enabling English-speaking people to understand and explore customs and traditions of the Tibetan people and also to serve as a brief introduction to the diasporic Tibetan youth. The book offers a brief and clear insight into the customs and traditions of Tibetan people such as smearing a black mark on babies, the funeral rites for the deceased, decorating a green barley sprout and a sheep's head on Tibetan New Year, performing Tibetan operas, the five schools of Tibetan Buddhism, festivals of Tibet and so forth. Tibetan customs and traditions are deeply related to the nomadic and agricultural lifestyle of the Tibetan people with the Bon religion and Buddhism at its core.

Each chapter in this book unfolds with a drawing that attempts to delineate the idea of the section. Wherever the titles of various books quoted in this text appear, they are italicized. Unfamiliar Tibetan terms are explained in footnotes where possible. Except for common Tibetan names, diacritics are used and other Tibetan terms are italicized and written in Wylie transliteration lest the phonetics might lead to incorrect orthography. The English translation is rendered in a simple register considering that the majority of the readers would

viii *A Hundred Customs and Traditions of Tibetan People*

be unacquainted with Tibetan customs and traditions. I have tried to maintain fidelity to the text and fluency of the translation though I cannot claim this work to be a literal translation. During the course of my translation, in the event of difficulty in understanding the Tibetan text, I sought help from elderly Tibetans who are the only bearers of Tibet's rich customs and traditions.

His Holiness the Dalai Lama describes Tibetan culture as a compassionate and peaceful culture which could soon become extinct. Tibetans inside Tibet and the diaspora Tibetan community are both confronted with the challenge to maintain their distinct identity [culture] in the face of strong mainstream assimilative pressures. In the case of exile Tibetans, this process is exacerbated as the land and environment – that gave birth to such customs and traditions are bifurcated. For how long will the Tibetans resist is a matter of will.

Lastly, the book in your hand owes its existence to our Director Geshe Lhakdor, who took great pains in verifying the English translation with the original Tibetan text. My thanks also go to Gyen Sangye Tendar, Ju Tenkyong, Wangdu Tsering la, Tsewang Bhuti and Dr. Chok Monlam for helping me by sharing their knowledge in the course of my translation. I thank my parents for their unstinting support. I would like to thank Hillary Williams from England for polishing the first four chapters and Akers Deborah from the United States for editing the remaining text. I also thank our house editor Katrina Moxey for proofreading the final draft. If there are any mistakes, they are entirely my own.

1

OFFERING SUBSTANCE

1. The White Scarf (*kha btags*)

Khatag is made up of two words: *kha* meaning 'mouth' and *btags* meaning 'to drape'. Originally, during an audience with a high lama or leader, before you make the request a clean white scarf is offered and draped to specially represent the purity of your speech. Gradually, scarves have become a unique ritual object, not only symbolizing one's highest reverence, but also happiness and sorrow. So Tibetans use *khatag* not only to represent auspicious occasions, but also inauspicious occasions. For example, during the death of a person and their funeral procession one end of a scarf is tied across the deceased and the other end is held by a selected man. This is known as guiding the path. This symbolizes that the deceased is being led towards a positive path.

White scarves have other uses. There is *dendar (gdan dar)* which family or friends drape across a traveler's bed after he leaves his house,

2 A Hundred Customs and Traditions of Tibetan People

and *nyenshel (rnyan shal)*, scarves that visitors to monasteries offer before the image or statue of enlightened beings and deities.

It is clear to all that when the white scarf is offered, it is draped around the neck of the recipient. If the person you are offering it to is your senior in age, a lama or leader, then the scarf should be offered gracefully and reverentially into their hands. It would be considered disrespectful to put it around their neck, particularly if a woman does so.

There are regional differences in the way scarves are offered. People from Lhasa offer the scarf by holding it above the person and then lowering it over their neck and downwards. Those from the Tsang region offer the scarf first from the person's neck, then upwards around their neck.

Traditionally in Tibet, white scarves were made of wool. Such as a better quality of scarf (*nang mdzod*), the second quality scarf (*a she*), an inferior scarf (*zub she*), *söd tag (bsod btags)* a kind of *zub she*. Nowadays, white scarves are made of silk of various qualities.

—◆◆—

2. Butter-flour (*phye mar*)

Butter-flour is an indispensable substance used by Tibetans on every auspicious occasion like *Losar* (Tibetan New Year), housewarmings and marriages. According to oral tradition, the offering of butter-flour and roasted wheat can be traced back to the time before the Dharma King Songtsen Gampo (569-650) and reflects the nomadic and agricultural lifestyle of Tibetans. It was not, however, as elaborate as it is today.

If someone raises doubts about the basis of thought behind this tradition and under what conditions this tradition originates, the slight influence of the Bon religion is apparent. This is because it is an indispensable item in Bon rituals, such as worshipping deities and securing good fortune. Along with the growth of the Bon religion, this tradition became widespread among the common people. It is thus clear that the idea behind this tradition of offering butter-flour and roasted wheat is directly linked to the Bon religion.

Secondly, it is related to the developmental stage of the ancient agricultural economy. Since Tibetans at that time relied exclusively on nomadic and agricultural work, it is safe to say that to honor this work, butter-flour and roasted wheat were arranged and displayed to express auspiciousness for good crops and abundant agricultural production, which in turn would lead to prosperity. The word *phye* means 'finely ground barley' (flour) and *mar* means 'butter'. Butter is considered the essential nomadic product.

Butter-flour and grains are displayed and offered in a double-sided wooden box (*'bo'*). Wheat (*gro*) or roasted wheat (*gro yos*) are put in one side of the box and roasted barley flour (tsampa) is put in the other side. The Tibetan word for wheat (*gro*) suggests luck and auspiciousness. The barley signifies agricultural work and the butter, which is tipped on the barley, signifies the nomadic product. Based on the ingredients involved in butter-flour, one can conclude that this custom has a deep relation to agricultural and nomadic production.

❖

3. Prayer Flags (*dar lcog*)

Wherever prayer flags are hanging, you can be certain a Tibetan lives nearby. Tibetans have a unique custom of hoisting prayer flags and long prayer banners on mountain tops, on their houses, in village squares, in forests and around monasteries and holy sites. *Dar* refers to cloth woven from cotton (*sring bal*) or a synthetic material of wool and nylon (*krang men*). *Lcog* refers to its upright posture (*tsog tsog*). The flags are therefore named after the material from which they are made and their shape. The great scholar Gedun Chophel (1905-1950), in his book *The White Annals* wrote that this tradition has been practiced since the days of early Tibetan kings and thus has a history of over one thousand years. He further wrote that "in every house, a pole flag is raised; this is also a unique Tibetan custom as it appears that

---

1 The box is painted with various designs such as dragons, wish-fulfilling jewels and the eight auspicious symbols

4 *A Hundred Customs and Traditions of Tibetan People*

originally it was used as a sign of warfare which gradually found its role in religious activities." This piece of writing tells us about the origin, stages of development and nature of the prayer flag. As Buddhism became widespread in Tibetan lives, ancient military signs, such as primitive flags and spears, transformed into the present practice of hoisting prayer flags, endowed with the profound Buddhist thinking of overcoming obstacles, dispelling miseries and enriching the energy that carries good fortune.

Tibetans raise beautiful colored flags on top of mountain peaks and rooftops; but it is not one's privilege to randomly hoist any color of flags. There are five different colors in prayer flags and these should be arranged without upsetting the order. The flags are arranged in a color sequence: blue on the top and then, white, red, green and yellow signifying the five external natural elements. Blue represents the sky, white represents the clouds, red represents fire, green represents water and yellow represents the earth. This is because the external world is the dwelling place for the beings inhabiting it. Tibetans believe that if there is harmony between the natural elements then the crops will be abundant, cattle will thrive and people will be blessed with longevity and merits, transforming this human world into a realm of peace, joy and happiness. If the balance or harmony is upset, then the human world will be full of sorrow and misery. According to the principles of Tibetan astrology, another explanation of the color sequence represents fire as red, earth as yellow, wood as green, water as blue and iron as white. Therefore, prayer flags are raised with special emphasis according to your nature. For instance, if your nature is fire, an importance is laid on the red prayer flag.

Prayer flags are printed with religious verses, mantras and animal figures. A popular design is the Fortune Prayer Flag or the Wind-horse. This has a horse printed in the centre and a tiger, lion, *garuda*[2] and dragon in each corner. It symbolizes victory over all. It is said that, because the tiger is the king of carnivores, the lion the king of

---

2   A mythical bird of great size that appears in both Buddhist and Hindu mythology

herbivores, the *garuda* the king of birds and the dragon the king of the sky, they are the four supreme animals and have the power to subdue others.

Also your actions, depicted in the form of the supreme horse [in this particular image, at the centre] suggest a journey from an evil path to a positive path. Thus, this horse, which is adorned with jewels at the back, represents the fulfillment of all the individual wishes. This is the genuine definition of the wind-horse.

Lately, because of the concept of riding the wind, people started writing wind-horse (*rlung rta*) instead of the original *klung rta*. Since prayer flags are raised into the sky and constantly flap in the wind, it seems the name wind-horse is so designated.

—•:•—

4. White Lines (*dkar thig*)

White lines showing directions and patterns signifying auspiciousness are drawn with chalk both inside and outside the house. In their daily life, Tibetans draw white lines to welcome somebody, to celebrate an auspicious occasion and even when a dead body is to be taken out. So the occasion determines the design of the drawing. The eight auspicious symbols are drawn to welcome high lamas, *tulkus*[3] and great leaders for religious ceremonies. A swastika is used for other common auspicious celebrations. From the house of the deceased, a straight white line is drawn on each side of the road to mark the way of the funeral procession.

In the lives of Tibetans, the tradition of drawing white lines is widespread, mainly because it represents prosperity and auspiciousness. White represents auspiciousness because Tibetans regard it as the color of goodness and excellence. For example, helping others – and other good deeds – are referred to as white deeds. Sincere or faithful friends and relatives are referred to as white souls. Therefore, the color and

---

3   An emanation of an earlier lama

6   *A Hundred Customs and Traditions of Tibetan People*

the patterns, such as the elaborate eight auspicious symbols and the swastika, all convey auspiciousness. Thus, this custom of drawing white lines has lasting imprints on the lives of Tibetans.

---

5. Five Color Rainbow (*'ja' tshon sna lnga*)

The rainbow, which is one of the perpetual occurrences in the sky, is said to be made of seven colors, but according to the Tibetan belief, it consists of only five colors. This may be based on the Tibetans deep faith in Buddhism and reverence for the five groups of Dakini: East Vajra Dakini, South Rinchen Dakini, West Padma Dakini, North Karma Dakini and Central Buddha Dakini. All are believed to be symbols of the five colors in the rainbow.

---

6. Decoration of Cookies (*sder kha*)

Tibetans have a custom of decorating cookies during *Losar* and other major functions. Cookies are also an indispensable item and are made not merely for feasting purposes, but also as an offering to the Three Jewels. It is a principal substance representing auspiciousness. Though I have not found any texts written about the origin of this custom, I did interview some elders and according to them it originates from the Bon religion, which used animal sacrifices. Buddhism transformed this into offering cookies to the Three Jewels. The cookies are made in shapes to represent parts of the human body, like thigh-bones represented by *khurkhog (khur khog)*, ribs represented by *nyashag (nya shag)*, small intestines represented by *mugthung (smug thung)*, large intestines represented by *bo lug (sbo lug)* and the heart represented by *pin tok (pin tog)*. So it is clear that in the beginning the cookies were for sacrificial offerings. However, now they represent auspiciousness. For example, the wheat from which cookies are prepared is known as *gro*

Offering Substance 7

zhib and so it has the meaning of *kha dro wa* meaning auspiciousness. These specially prepared cookies are fried in butter or oil. In Tibetan something "oily" is regarded as a positive aspect. There are sayings in Tibetan like "a man with an oily (glowing) face" (*mi snum zhag dod po*) and "an oily (glowing) region" (*lung pa snum zhag dod po*). The cookies are arranged in a clean dish with fruits, nuts and other confections. An odd number of cookies is used (three, five, seven or nine) to suggest auspiciousness. They may be placed face down or up depending on the region of Tibet. In Central Tibet they will be placed face down and in Tsang face up.

❖

7. Green Barley Sprouts and Sheep's Head (*lo phud / lug mgo*)

During *Losar*, there is a custom of offering green barley sprouts *(lo phud)* and a sheep's head *(lug mgo)*. This custom originates out of the actual daily life of Tibetans. Since Tibetans at that time relied exclusively on agricultural and nomadic products, everyone hoped for a good harvest. These offerings symbolizing auspiciousness during the *Losar* convey the respect and value Tibetans attribute to their agricultural and nomadic work. Before *Losar*, barley is planted in a small clean pot so that when *Losar* comes it will have sprouted and small green shoots will have appeared. It is considered as the best crop of the year and decorated on the altar. If the sprouts grow well, it is already an indication that the harvest will be a good one.

In the Tibetan language *lug mgo* (sheep's head) and *lo 'go* (beginning of a year) have similar pronunciations. As a result, at the beginning of Tibetan *Losar*, a sheep's head *(lug mgo)* is decorated as a symbol of auspiciousness. It used to be the custom to eat a sheep's head on the first day of *Losar*. Some say this custom represents a strong influence from the Bon religion's practice of animal sacrifice. According to another folklore, four Tibetan ministers brought food, *chang* (see 87) and *shazug* (one fourth of a carcass) for a meeting with the queen that took place in the

8 *A Hundred Customs and Traditions of Tibetan People*

centre of a meadow under a walnut tree near Wothang Lake to discuss the possibility of the King taking a Chinese and a Nepalese princess as wives. The *shazug* they had brought were found to be a complete sheep's carcass and this was considered to be very auspicious. The offering of a sheep's carcass thus became a custom symbolizing prosperity, but now, for convenience, only a head is offered.

---

8. Smoke Offering (*bsang*)

Tibetans are very particular about smoke offerings. On top of almost every Tibetan home, there is a smoke offering vase. Such vases are also found along the sides of paths used for circumambulation and at the entrance to temples. People make 'mountain smoke offering' and 'smoke offering to *nagas*'. Smoke offerings are made to receive lamas, *tulkus* and other great leaders. I have not seen clear accounts that tell when this custom of smoke offering got started and how it originated. The Tibetan scholar Chapel Tsetan Phuntsok writes, "The smoke offering custom is an indispensable practice in propitiating worldly deities. Historically, it is said to be a preliminary ritual before invoking deities with an intention to dispel the uncleanliness and impurities of the human realm." An early Bon text entitled *A Commentary of Yongtse* describes the descent of King Nyatri Tsenpo from the heaven realm together with three other divine Bonpo priests, Yangal *(ya ngal)*, Tsemi *(mtse mi)* and Tsomi *(tso mi)*. The text reads "...And the reverend Father spoke, 'when a divine being descends down to the human realm, filled with filth and obscuration, Yangal shall lead the way. Escorted to the right by Tsemi and to the left by Tsomi, Yangal will burn incense to purify the road.'" Therefore, when deities and gods are invited, purifying smoke offerings are made to remove contaminations and defilements. The Bon religion has influenced this practice and it has been more than 2000 years since its spread in Tibet.

Offering Substance 9

9. Mountain Cairns with Prayer Flags (*la btsas*)

Cairns here refers to heaps of stone with flags that are erected on top of mountain passes that people cross and are meant to propitiate deities or positive spirits. According to Tibetan scholars, *la* means mountain and *btsas* most likely means a tax paid when visiting a sacred peak.

The custom of offering prayers to the deities relates deeply to travels. Since Tibetans live mostly in high altitude and mountainous regions and in ancient times, horses, mules, yaks and *dzo* (a cross between a yak and a cow) were the main means of transportation, so most Tibetans had to walk. Crossing the mountain passes was a long and arduous journey. Therefore, when people crossed one mountain pass, they considered it one tiring task of a journey accomplished and they would collect some fresh stones and then leave a small quantity of food on it as a kind of tax and offering. This was done for two reasons: first, to create an auspicious circumstance for the crossing of the pass; secondly, to create a positive thought for other long-distance travelers behind them who might have been devoid of food for many days. But later the practice changed into propitiating deities. As people crossing the pass keep on piling stones, it became huge and then people started putting up flags and propitiating deities. There are also people who believe that, initially, mountain passes with stone cairns and prayer flags were regarded as boundaries for each region. If someone had to travel through these passes, he or she would have to pay taxes in the form of gifts, which later changed into propitiating deity practices.

2
CUSTOMS AND TRADITIONS

10. Traditional Beliefs about Sights Seen when Traveling (*lam rtags rtsi srol*)

Tibetans have a tradition of paying great attention to sights seen on the road during wedding ceremonies and during the start of a traveler's journey. For example, while receiving the bride and bridegroom, or when someone begins their travels, if the following sights are seen then it is considered a sign of good luck and success in work: people carrying firewood on their backs, a water vessel filled with water, a traveler beautifully dressed in fine clothing and ornaments, someone wearing a complete white traditional dress *(chu pa)*, or a herd of animals carrying a full load. According to the popular saying, "A wolf on your right, a fox on your left or the rear view of a rabbit will bring you auspiciousness." On the other hand, it is considered inauspicious to see an empty water vessel, someone carrying an empty bamboo basket on their back, a

12 *A Hundred Customs and Traditions of Tibetan People*

horse with an empty saddle, a woman with unkept hair, a sick person, a funeral procession, a woman not wearing an apron, or a monk, etc. Therefore, different methods are used to ward off misfortunes.

—◆:◆—

11. The Custom of Raising Thumbs and Little Fingers (*mthe bong ker srol*)

In Tibetan culture, the custom of raising one's thumb or little finger is a way of expressing acceptance or dislike and requests or pleas. The thumb is raised to express appreciation of good work. However, in matters of disappointment and unpleasantness, Tibetans raise their little finger to express dislike. In matters of desperation and helplessness, people make a request and plead by raising both their thumbs.

—◆:◆—

12. The Custom of Removing the Right Sleeve (*phu thung g.yas pa phud srol*)

In nomadic and agricultural areas, it is common to see a Tibetan in traditional dress with their right arm out of their right sleeve. There are three reasons for this. First, in production labor and other work the right hand is used for most of the heavy work, so for comfort and higher labor productivity it is not covered by the sleeve of the *chupa*. Secondly, in Tibet, there is a large variation in temperatures throughout the day, so wearing the *chupa* in this way allows for temperature regulation. Thirdly, placing the hanging sleeve over the right shoulder is a mark of respect used when meeting lamas, elders and scholars.

—◆:◆—

13. The Customs of Joining the Palms òf the Hands and Folding the Fingers (*thal mo sbyar ba'i srol*)

In temples and monasteries, before the representations of Buddha's body, speech and mind, Tibetans join their palms to pray and make a wish. When meeting someone of higher position, Tibetans will join their palms as a mark of respect. The joining of the palms suggests deep faith and expresses reverence toward others.

There is also a custom of folding your four fingers and thumb and showing them to someone, which means, 'shut up' and 'it is none of your business'. If one were to do this, it would be disrespectful and insulting.

—◆—

14. The Custom of Referring to the Day and Date[1] When Travelling (*phyogs la thon skabs gza' tshes lta ba'i srol*)

The custom of consulting various astrological texts before setting out on a journey originates from the astrological tradition. Journeys are considered important undertakings by Tibetans. Warding off misfortunes and obstacles and having success in the task ahead depends largely on what day the person chooses to begin their journey. Great attention is paid to selecting an auspicious day on which to start the journey. If, however, a traveler fails to depart on an auspicious day, they may take a few steps in the direction of their destination on that day, as a means of averting misfortune. If a traveler makes a journey on Sunday, it is considered an inappropriate day for travel in astrological texts and one may encòunter difficulties. Thus, people avoid traveling on Sundays. A person strictly avoids traveling on days

---

1 The twelve lunar months of a Tibetan year have approximately 354 solar days. Tibetan astrology describes the auspicious and inauspicious characteristics of each day.

14 *A Hundred Customs and Traditions of Tibetan People*

of *chutsag (chu tshags).*[2] If the traveler begins on this day it is said that many inauspicious signs might happen like a horse dying and a saddle breaking. If the traveler is heading in the direction of *bumtong (bum stongs),*[3] he turns back and proceeds toward the Tsang direction *(gtsang phyogs)*[4] as an immediate act to remove any obstacles *bumtong* might portend.

—◆—

15. Soul Day, Life Force Day and Life Foe Day
(*bla gza', srog gza' and gshed gza'*)

Before Tibetans begin any task, they refer to their soul day *(bla gza')*, life force day *(srog gza')* and life foe day *(gshed gza')*. This custom originated from various astrological texts. People make sure that they begin their new task on a soul day or a life force day. As per the oral tradition, if one begins a task on a soul day or a life force day one will achieve success and glory. Important work should always be initiated on a life force day or a soul day and there is no custom of carrying out important work on a life foe day. As it is written in astrology texts, "carry out your work, when your soul day or life force day is high, but avoid any work on a life foe day."

By comparing the following table (see Table 1) with the year of your birth, one can learn the day of your life force day, soul day and life foe day.

---

2 The second day and every six days after it of the twelve Tibetan months.

3 According to Tibetan Astrology, there are four *bum stongs* in four directions. Depending upon the movements of the solar planets, one of the directions is considered inauspicious.

4 Tibetan Astrology maintains that *gtsang phyogs* is an auspicious direction in which to carry out ceremonies such as marriage and funerals. This auspicious direction changes after every year.

YEAR \ DAY	Soul Day	Life Foe Day	Life Force Day
Mouse	Wednesday	Tuesday	Saturday
Ox	Saturday	Wednesday	Thursday
Tiger	Thursday	Saturday	Friday
Hare	Thursday	Saturday	Friday
Dragon	Sunday	Wednesday	Thursday
Snake	Tuesday	Friday	Wednesday
Horse	Tuesday	Friday	Wednesday
Sheep	Friday	Monday	Thursday
Monkey	Friday	Thursday	Tuesday
Bird	Friday	Thursday	Tuesday
Dog	Monday	Wednesday	Thursday
Pig	Wednesday	Tuesday	Saturday

Table 1

16. Prostration (*phyag 'tshal*)

In places inhabited by Tibetans, it is a common sight to see people doing prostrations. Many foreigners fail to understand the meaning behind prostrations. They wonder why Tibetans have to endure such hardships and they view it with amazement.

Speaking from the point of view of a person performing the prostrations, and speaking from the point of religious belief there are definite objectives for enduring such hardships. It is a means to purify all negative actions, to dispel all obscurations and to enter the path of liberation. In order to achieve Buddhahood, prostration is a special homage paid through the body, speech and mind.[5] Because

---
5 Throughout the prostration one should maintain a strong state of concentration, faith and sincerity.

16 *A Hundred Customs and Traditions of Tibetan People*

of such objectives, one generates enthusiasm without being bothered by hardships.

Prostrations are of two types: full-length prostration and half prostration.[6] A full-length prostration can be seen in Lhasa on Barkor Street, on the way to the outer path of the city *(gling skor)* and in front of the Jokhang temple. Some pilgrims travel to Lhasa and Mt. Kailash from distant areas like Tsongon *(mtsho sngon)* by performing full-length prostrations. A number of prostrations may personally be prescribed such as a hundred prostrations, one thousand prostrations or one hundred thousand prostrations as a means to purify one's defilements. A half prostration involves bending the knees and touching the floor with the same hand movements. As a mark of respect, three half-length prostrations are performed before high lamas and the three representations of the Buddha's body, speech and mind.

—◆—

17. The Custom of Mutual Care
(phan tshun sems 'khur byed pa'i lam srol)

In times of happiness or sorrow, Tibetans have a noble tradition of showing their love and concern for each other. At the start of any important work, relatives, neighbors and sincere friends visit each other's houses, bringing tea, *chang,* a white scarf and other gifts as a symbol of auspiciousness and prosperity. There is also a custom of helping one another by providing labor during the construction of houses and at harvest time. If any misfortunes fall on a family, relatives and neighbors rush to offer their condolences with tea, *chang* and whatever help they can offer. Tibetans attach great importance to helping others, showing

---

6 Prostration is done by touching one's palms together – fingers outstretched and thumbs tucked in – firstly to the top of the head, secondly to the mid-brow area, thirdly to the throat and fourthly to the heart. Ensure that five parts of the body, the forehead, two knees, and two palms of the hands, touch the ground. Then one lays face down on the ground. For full-length prostrations, one stretches out with hands fully extended in front of one's head with the above postures.

concern and maintaining harmonious relationships in their daily lives. A common decoration in Tibetan homes is a drawing of the Four Harmonious Friends (See. 40), which emphasize harmonious relations.

—◆:◆—

18. The Custom of Removing Hat, Scratching Head and Sticking Out Tongue (*zhva phud nas mgo brad dang lce snar snar byed pa'i srol*)

Traditionally, when Tibetans meet a high official or someone they respect, they remove their hats, scratch their heads and stick out their tongues. As per the origin of this custom, folklore suggests that the 42nd King of Tibet, the Demon Lang Darma (815-842), had horns and a black tongue like a cow. When people meet a high official or someone they respect, they remove their hats and scratch their heads to show they do not have horns and stick out their tongues to prove it is not black therefore revealing, in both actions, that they are not a demon. Gradually, this became a custom signifying respect. However, the custom now no longer exists in cities; it is more prevalent in remote villages.

—◆:◆—

19. Smearing a Black Mark on a Newborn Infant (*phru gu dmar 'byar la sre nag byug pa'i srol*)

When Tibetans take their baby out, it is a common sight to see a black mark smeared on the nose of the infant. According to traditional Tibetan belief, the mark is a means of protecting babies from harm and it is intended to make the newborn child look unpleasant so as not to draw the attention of spirits and demons who might inflict harm and curses. It is hard to express whether spirits and demonic harm exist or not. A more practical explanation for this custom may be that if babies look beautiful, they will be touched by many people, increasing their chance of contracting a contagious disease. It is understood that

18   *A Hundred Customs and Traditions of Tibetan People*

Tibetans keep their good qualities and values secret, with the view that it will prevent curses and aversions arising in the minds of others. There is no doubt that this is a wise ancient method.

---

20. Rubbing Money on Your Clothes before Giving It to Others (*dngul rang gos thog phyis nas gzhan la sprod pa'i srol*)

Tibetans place great emphasis on not letting their good luck slip away so that they will continue to be blessed with fortune, glory and wealth, and merit. People keep charm boxes in their houses and perform rituals for bringing luck and good fortune. When a Tibetan gives away money, they gently rub it on their clothes to symbolize that even though they are giving their money away, they will not lose their luck and good fortune. For the same reason, when giving roasted barley flour and grains to others, a handful is always taken back.

---

21. The Custom of Swearing (Taking Oaths) (*mna' skyel*)

The custom of taking an oath in front of the Three Jewels is known as swearing (*mna' skyel*). There are different interpretations regarding the meaning of the term 'swear'. Some scholars interpret the term as *sna*, which refers to a nose that stays straight on the face. The act of swearing is a dividing line that separates truth from falsehood. In the past it was called *sna* (nose), but, over time, it gradually changed to *mna'* (swear).

The origin of the swearing custom is strongly related to the Bon religion. This is because in former times, while taking an oath or making a pledge, an animal sacrifice, red offerings[7] and smearing blood across

---

7   The offerings made to the deities and gods in the form of blood and flesh.

Customs and Traditions 19

the mouth were the conditions of swearing. Additionally, in earlier times, when there was no proper legal system, the only way to get to the truth of a matter in life was by relying on swearing and taking pledges to sort out disputes between people, households and groups.

The swearing of oaths has left deep imprints on the lives of Tibetans. There is a saying "an oath is like a tiny dew drop, it is small yet it makes the shoe wet." It is said that the negative consequences of swearing are severe. People who are bound by faith and promises do not transgress their pledges and those who transgress are considered the most inferior. The act of swearing is highly regarded by Tibetans and it is the yardstick to measure whether the person's actions are sincere or not. Most people do not swear often and never for trivial reasons. If someone is prepared to swear to a matter, they are believed to be telling the truth.

3

TIBETAN PERFORMING ARTS

22. Tibetan Opera (*lha mo*)

Tibetan opera has a long history. Murals in ancient monasteries, dating from before the 14th century, show scenes of early Tibetan opera art form, known as 'The White-Mask'. Gradually, because of political, economical and cultural developments, the tradition of Tibetan opera has flourished and the ancient art of performing – such as solo performances and the dance of the Wild Yaks *('brong rtsed)* – have progressively become a central piece of Tibet's performing arts.

Tibetan opera *(Ache Lhamo)* was created by Yogi Thangtong Gyalpo (1361-1485) in the year 1385. During the reign of the great 5th Dalai Lama (1612-1682) the repertoire of Tibetan opera grew and a rich art of story-telling dealing with a wide range of subjects developed. The features of Tibetan opera are: each opera tells a complete story, there is a great variation of tone in the singing, and the dancers move in a relaxed way and maintain a composed expression.

22 *A Hundred Customs and Traditions of Tibetan People*

With the development of Tibetan opera, more than twenty different kinds of slow and fast ways of singing the *Namthar* (the narratives, in verse form, sung by the performers in a fast chant) developed to represent the slow and fast movements, and the diverse characters. The purpose of these is to express the feelings of diverse characters in the opera performances and to generate their mental state.

The opera is generally performed by dividing it into three parts. First, there is a prelude where a hunter *(rngon pa)* performs the introductory rites. Next, the performance of the opera itself follows, and finally there is the epilogue, which features the concluding dance signifying the auspiciousness of the occasion. At the end of the opera, during the curtain call, the actors conclude with a dance and sponsors and audience members offer gifts as tokens of appreciation for the performance.

A large number of opera texts have been lost, but there are more than ten existing texts; although, only eight are considered classical opera texts. The themes of Tibetan opera are derived from historical events, lives of enlightened beings and folktales. The titles of the eight classical Tibetan operas are Zugkyi Nyima, Drowa Sangmo, Gyasa Kongjo, Nangsa Wöbum, Pema Wöbar, Chung Dhonyö and Dhundup, Chogyal Drimey Kunden and Chögyal Norsang. The titles refer to the names of the people upon whose lives the operas are based.

—◆—

23. The Role of Masks in Tibetan Opera
(*ras 'bag so so'i don gyi bstan bya*)

During the performance of any section of Tibetan opera, there is a tradition of wearing different colored masks. Tibetan opera has two different traditions: the white mask of Tashi Zhöpa[1] that spread earlier and the dark blue mask of the later tradition.

From the white goatee up to the white hair, the white mask of Tashi Zhöpa represents the distinct facial features of Yogi Thangtong

---

1 Good Luck Dance from the Shol area of Lhasa, Tibet

Tibetan Performing Arts 23

Gyalpo (see 22). The hair of a white goat is attached to the mask, and represents the old age of Thangtong Gyalpo, whose gray hair, beard and eyelashes seem to compete with the radiance of a white conch shell. In Tibetan, this ornamental goat hair is called *tshe ring* (longevity) and *g.yang chags* (good fortune); longevity is for the elderly people, wishing them to be free of suffering, and good fortune is for the youths and adults, blessing them with wealth and wisdom.

The mask of the later tradition of Tibetan opera is dark blue, signifying a wrathful and heroic nature. This is because the white mask worn by the hunter earlier during the prelude had changed to navy blue. The dark blue color of the mask originates from the visit to Yardrog *(yar 'brog)* by the great yogi Drugpa Kunleg (1455-1529). When he spoke to the fishermen of the region he said, "You, fishermen of Yardrog have a bluish complexion similar to that of the wrathful deity Vajrapani.[2]" Moreover, the mask of a hunter is richly adorned with ornaments that echo the eight auspicious symbols (see 43). The dark blue mirror on the mask represents the vase of treasure. The richly painted mouth, eyes, eyebrows, cheeks and throat represent the lotus flower. A nose ornament adorned with multi-colored silk threads represents endless knots. A design of the sun and moon on the forehead represents the dharma wheel. A mother-of-pearl dangling below the nose represents the right-coiled white conch. The section of the mask that covers the center of the forehead to the ears is adorned with a silk brocade which represents the two golden fish facing each other. Ornamented with precious jewels is the *thor cog*[3] and patterns of dogs' noses (upward curling spirals) at its top represent the parasol. Finally, a background cloth made of multicolored silk brocade represents the victory banner.

The red mask with black eyebrows and a moustache represents manhood and the graceful nature of the princely father. The green mask of the great mother represents the beauty and elegance of women. The yellowish white colored hermit's mask with a white eyebrow and

---

2 Buddhist deity Chakna Dorjee known in Sanskrit as Vajrapani

3 An upright figure that extends above the mask or the crown of the mask

24 *A Hundred Customs and Traditions of Tibetan People*

a moustache represents the facial features of the above mentioned yogi Thangtong Gyalpo. The half-black and half-white mask of the Yama-Ganti represents the character's two-faced nature or duplicity.

---

24. Sacred Tantric Dance (*cham*)

In most Tibetan monasteries, there is a tradition of performing sacred tantric dances called *Cham,* which are greatly loved by the Tibetan people. It is estimated that a long period of time has elapsed since the beginning of this tradition of performing sacred tantric dances. *The Great Performance of Tsang,* written by Ngawang Thupten states that sacred tantric dances are an important religious activity at monasteries in Tibet. During the early dissemination of Buddhism in Tibet under the reign of Trisong Deutsen (742-797), Tibet's 38th king, and other early Tibetan kings, yogis performed the sacred tantric dance to empty themselves of the concepts of ordinary beings[4] and transcend into the state of the wrathful personal deity *(yi dam).* They carried weapons and various symbolic attributes of deities in their hands. It was considered part of the secret tantric rituals and was not for public spectacle. In the course of time – some 900 years ago in the case of the hagiography of Ache Nangsa – the sacred tantric dance of the Gyaltse Nenying monastery was opened for everyone – including both monks and lay people. The inner meaning of the sacred tantric dances originated from the activities of yogis. As per the nature and the distinctive qualities of particular tenets of Buddhist schools, the dances signify the arrival of *bodhisattvas,*[5] peaceful *dakinis* and the wrathful personal deities, who are thought to confer blessings to the spectators.

---

4   The concepts of ordinary beings share three delusions
5   A being who, having developed the Awakening Mind, devotes their life to the task of achieving Buddhahood for the sake of all sentient beings

25. Western Tibetan Dance (*stod gzhas*)

Töshey (Western Tibetan dance) is a song and dance adapted from the Ngari region and is also a combination of dance and melodious musical instruments of Tibet's common folk. It can also be called the song and dance of the Tö region. During the dance, as the beginning movements of *töshey*, the male dancers lift their legs high enough to forcefully stomp on the ground. The actual male dance steps resemble an arrow being pulled on a bow. The dance steps for women resemble the spinning of yarn for weaving. As per the related written materials *töshey* is a blend of song, dance and melodious music, which is loved, even by the glorious youth. This kind of dance is also known as the Tibetan Lute Dance of Lhasa *(lha sa'i sgra snyan zhabs bro)*.

Depending upon the tradition of performing *töshey*, it can further be classified into two groups: northern Tö and southern Tö. The songs and dances of southern Tö are classified as slow, relaxed and melodious. On the other hand, the songs and dances of northern Tö are defined as heroic, energetic and composed. After the spread of *töshey* in Lhasa, it can be classified in two. The *dal gzhas* (slow song) has become known as *rgyang gzhas* (very slow way of dancing) and the dance that accompanies fast music is known as *mgyogs gzhas* (fast song).

With the spread of *töshey* in the province of Ü-Tsang, the tone, pitch and tune of this specific western Tibetan dance was slightly influenced or changed by the characteristics of Ü-Tsang songs and dances. According to a few reputable scholars, *töshey* refers to a song of praise.

❖

26. Nangma (*nang ma*)

There is a lot of research on *nangma,* and one can find quite a number of research papers written about it. There are people who hold the view that it is 'court music', but I feel that this is not the case. *Nangma* is a musical genre that developed from the gradual change of Tibet's traditional folk songs and music. The elegant and melodious tune of

26 *A Hundred Customs and Traditions of Tibetan People*

nangma and the dignified and graceful body movements are typical of the Tibetan people and it is therefore widespread in Ü-Tsang.

The performance of *nangma* is divided into three sections: the prelude *('jog)*, the middle or slow section *(rgyang gzhas)* and the finale or fast section *('khrug gzhas)*.

The prelude of a *nangma* song is purely instrumental: it has neither voice nor dance. The sweet and melodious tune of the slow section *(rgyang gzhas)* is considered to be the essence of *nangma*. There is not much dancing in this section, but a body posture that embodies elegance and respect is assumed. The singer often displays reverence by prostrating his body or joining his palms. The quick change of rhythms in the third section offers joy and this section is the fastest part of the *nangma* performance. *Töshey* and *nangma* have influenced each other in many ways. In particular, the dance movements in *nangma* originate mostly from *töshey*.

Most of the verses of *nangma* follow six-syllable lines conveying the message of prosperity. The musical instruments used in *nangma* are the six-stringed Tibetan lute, the flute, fiddle *(piwang)*, dulcimer, *dal chen* (similar to a Chinese fiddle), *gan chag* and the small bell *(ling shang)*.

—◆—

27. Round Dance *(sgor gzhas)*

In a round dance, the dancers join hands to form a circle. Men and women assemble in one place and with great joy and laborious expression, men initiate the song and women sing the concluding parts, or vice versa. In the major villages of Domey and Ü-Tsang provinces, round-dancing is a popular dance form. It has its own unique features and does not need any musical instruments. It begins with the singing of a slow song, followed by lively and vigorous dancing. Round dancing, in general, is uniform in Tibet, but depending upon the diverse characteristics of each region, it can be regionally classified, for example Tsang round dance, Lhoka round dance and Tö round dance. In each region, a slight variation in tone, lyrics and movements are evident.

---

28. Victory Dance (*rgyal gzhas*)

Victory dance is a unique folk dance performed in the Dingri, Tsang and Sakya region. This art has been flourishing since the reign of King Songtsen Gampo (569-650A.D.). During the performance men dress themselves in the costume of ancient rulers, while women adorn themselves in their Tsang regional dress. The lyrics are profound and wish prosperity for all. While dancing, there is a shift from relaxed body movements to the more vigorous movements which have specific regional characteristics. Once the dance begins, it continues for a long time and in some cases it lasts for a whole day.

---

29. Drum Dance (*bro*)

Drum dance *(bro)* is performed in a graceful manner and uses a wide range of tempos. In Chamdo, it is known as '*ral pa*' (drums and cymbals are used to accompany the songs) and in Ü-Tsang it is called '*bro gzhas*'. The performance of the drum dance is at its liveliest when accompanied by a furious tempo of beating drums and clashing cymbals. Men carry cymbals in their hands while women carry drums and move from a slow to a fast pace, exuding the dance platform with increasing joy. As the pace of the dance quickens, the men strike their cymbals on their right hands and the women beat their drums and artfully display their body movements. The dance of drums and cymbals offers great variations in movement and coordination, which arouses an unstoppable feeling of wonder, joy and serenity among the audience.

28 A Hundred Customs and Traditions of Tibetan People

The drum dance of Tsang is performed mostly in a series of sections. In between these sections, performers make commentaries by beating drums and singing songs. Their dancing imitates deer running in the field or birds pecking for food on the ground.

In the Lhasa and Lhoka regions the drum dance has a dance between sections that depicts the building of the Samye monastery. The dance has the characteristics of beauty and gracefulness and an expression of workers working laboriously.

4

TYPES OF DESIGN

30. The Golden Pinnacle (*gan ji ra*)

The reason for golden pinnacles made of gold and bronze on top of monasteries, temples, and palaces in Tibet is not merely for decoration; they have deep symbolic meanings. [All are uniformly comprised of five symbolic parts, stacked on top of each other] and represent the five Buddha families. At the bottom, the shape of a lotus represents Amitabha (Buddha of boundless life). Above that, the shape of a bell symbolizes Amogasiddhi (Buddha of unfailing protection). The shape of a wheel represents Variocana (belonging to the sun). The shape of a vase represents Akshobhya (Buddha of the immovable one) and the shape of a jewel represents Ratnasambhava (Buddha of the jewel born).

30 *A Hundred Customs and Traditions of Tibetan People*

31. The Dharma Wheel with Stag and Deer
(*ri dvags chos 'khor*)

A common figure on top of monasteries, the dharma wheel flanked by two deer is an unusual figure which signifies attraction toward Buddhadharma by all sentient beings as disciples. To explain it in detail, the three parts of the wheel are symbols of the Three Higher Trainings and the Three Baskets: the hub symbolizes ethical morality and Vinaya, the rim represents concentration and Sutra,[1] and the eight spokes represent wisdom and Abhidharma.

The male and female deer staring single-pointedly at the tip of the dharma wheel suggest that regardless of an individual embracing Buddhist doctrine or any other religion their ultimate goal is to attain the three exalted bodies of a Buddha. The path to tread is the supreme path shown by the Buddha, which indicates there is no other way than the Three Higher Trainings. In reality, the eight spokes of the wheel signify the noble eight-fold path[2] and the entire teachings of Buddha. The male and the female deer signify means and knowledge. In reality, in order to achieve enlightenment, a union of means and knowledge is needed. This represents a profound Buddhist tradition.

---

32. Cylindrical Banners of Black Yak Hair (*thug*)

Cylindrical banners are made from black yak hair and metal. The tridents (which are called "the blazing mountains") extend from the crown of the cylindrical banners. Cylindrical banners are erected on top of monasteries to mark the abode of a particular guardian deity. They also provide information about the guardian deity that the monastery propitiates as its protector. It is not one's privilege to raise cylindrical banners. It must be consecrated by a special ceremony involving the

---

1   *Sutra* is a Sanskrit word and it refers to exoteric teachings of the Buddha
2   The noble eight-fold path includes right view, thought, speech, action, livelihood, effort, mindfulness and concentration

Types of Design 31

placing of an axle *(srog shing)* in the centre of the banner and reciting a sacred incantation. These cylindrical banners are mostly black but, depending on the color of the guardian deity, they may also be white or red.

It is believed that black yak hair is used because a Hindu priest who embraced the Buddhist doctrine once offered a lock of his hair to Buddhadharma. Scientifically, cylindrical banners help monastic buildings avoid lightening.

33. Awnings (*sham bu*)

Tibetans have a custom of hanging small awnings on their doors and windows. [The awnings are pleated, and the number of pleats is normally uneven.] Old awnings are regularly replaced with new ones, especially on the eve of *Losar* and for wedding ceremonies. I have not found any written materials expressing why these awnings are put up, however according to the elderly people, they say these awnings are put up to suggest prosperity, auspiciousness, and new awnings are raised during *Losar* and auspicious gatherings. If someone dies or there is a catastrophe, the awnings are removed as an expression of grief.

Secondly, we can say for sure, these awnings are for decoration. Depending upon the financial status, rich families put up awnings made of silk, while poorer families use cotton. Thirdly, the architraves of doors and windows are often beautifully painted, and the awning protects these colors from fading. In the Tsang region, folded awnings are called *char yol* (rain curtain) and thus we can gain a brief understanding of their purpose.

34. Victory Banner (*rgyal mtshan*)

In Tibet, it is common to see a victory banner – located on top of temples, monasteries and shrines – made out of gold, bronze and silk.

32 *A Hundred Customs and Traditions of Tibetan People*

Many people are not fully aware of the purpose of erecting victory banners. Though the victory banner can be made of gold, bronze or colored flags, speaking from its true nature, it is a banner signifying victory over all disagreements, disharmonies, and hindrances. Wrapped around the upper part of the victory banner, there can either be three or nine folded silk valances. Three folds represent the victory banner of the protector deity Vaishravana *(rnam sras)*;[3] nine folds represent the nine good signs. These victory banners often have the images of an eagle in the body of a lion, a crocodile with the tail of a white conch, and a fish's head on the body of an otter.

◆◆◆

35. The Tenfold Powerful One
(*rnam bcu dbang ldan*)

Written in stacked Lantsa[4] characters, the Kalachakra seed syllable, or the tenfold powerful one, is a unique symbol of the Kalachakra mantra HAM KSHA MA LA VA RA YA. At the base of the celestial palace are the mandalas of earth, water, fire and air represented by the four Kalachakra seed syllables of LA, VA, RA and YA. Above this, and stacked together, are the three syllables MA, KSHA and HAM. MA symbolizes Mount Meru and the celestial palace itself. KSHA represents the enlightened body, speech and mind of the resident deities. HAM refers to the deities of the mandala of enlightened wisdom. The crescent moon, the red sun, and the flame represent the body, speech and mind of the deities of the mandala of great bliss. It is also said that they represent the residence and the resident deities *(rten brten pa'i lha rnams)*.

In the explanations of the Kalachakra tenfold powerful written by Lhasa *Cheng guan qu,* "The non-dualistic Kalachakra tenfold powerful

---

3   The god of wealth or king of mountain deities who guards the northern quarters

4   Lantsa is an Indian Buddhist script, probably of late Pala origin, derived from Sanskrit. Although certain scholars date it as late as the seventeenth century, it was used in Nepal until recent history. It is specifically used for mantra syllables and the titles of sacred texts

one is the five supports: air, fire, earth, water and Mount Meru. The form and the formless god realms and the sun and the moon, are the four waverings and the tenth Garuda. The use of the tenfold powerful one as an ornament in a house represents auspiciousness and prosperity."

◆:◆

36. The Eight Auspicious Substances
(*bkra shis rdzas brgyad*)

The eight substances considered to bring good fortune are as follows: mirror, ghiwang,[5] yogurt, durva grass, bilwa fruit, right-coiled conch, cinnabar and mustard seeds.

The mirror represents receiving auspicious blessings so that all sentient beings are able to enjoy the pure dharma without obstruction due to the actualization of the unobstructed primordial wisdom of the Buddha.

Ghiwang is a supreme medicine, which represents the realization of emptiness and the cure for all sicknesses of afflictive emotions and the sufferings that have arisen from the three poisons.[6]

Yogurt represents the pacification of the three poisons and the attainment of Buddhahood through the realization of the highest wisdom.

The durva grass is a symbol of long life. It brings an end to the cycle of birth and death caused by the three poisons and leads to the attainment of the immortal state of Vajra-being (Vajrasattava).

The bilva fruit represents the attainment of the highest essence of enlightenment, i.e. Buddhahood, through the infallible truth of the laws of cause and effect.

The right-coiled conch represents the authentic teaching of the three vehicles of Buddhism.

---

5 Ghiwang is a Chinese word meaning a kind of gallstone found in cattle. It is used in Tibetan medicine

6 According to Buddhist teaching, the three poisons are attachment, hatred and delusion

34 *A Hundred Customs and Traditions of Tibetan People*

The cinnabar represents dominion over the glory and the wealth of *samsara* and *nirvana* by the great rule of Dharma.

Mustard seeds represent victory over demons, obstacles and hindrances, through acquiring mastery in power and strength.

---

37. The Swastika with the Sun and Moon
(*nyi zla g.yung drung*)

Tibetans are extremely fond of the drawing of a swastika with a sun and moon at its top. One can see this drawing everywhere in Tibet, not only inside and outside the house and on doors, but also on the traditional dress and the ornamented otter-skin. It is not just an external decoration, but shares a far deeper relation with the tradition of the Bon religion. In the rites for bringing luck and prosperity, it states, "May the sun of life never set and illuminate forever; may the waxing moon of luck increase forever; may our race remain pure, firm like the swastika itself; may the joy and happiness of today be blessed forever." The swastika combined with a crescent and a disc (the sun and moon) represents many auspicious circumstances such as longevity, the perseverance of one's race and good fortune.

---

38. Coiled Jewel (*nor bu dga' 'khyil*)

Generally, people of every nationality love jewels. Tibetans consider jewels a benchmark to measure integrity. Good human beings and valuable objects are always praised and referred to as jewels. Under such perceptions, the followers of Buddhadharma, using their intelligence and creativity have drawn the design of coiled jewels and fixed a symbolic meaning to it. There are usually three different kinds of coiled jewels: two-colored, three-colored and four-colored. The two-colored coiled jewels symbolize means and knowledge. The three-colored coiled jewels refer to the three types of persons.[7] The four-colored coiled jewels represent the four joys: common joy, supreme joy, special joy and innate joy.

—◆—

39. The Six Signs of Long Life (*tshe ring drug skor*)

"The six signs of long life" is the name of a marvelous drawing found commonly in the houses of Tibetans. The origin of this drawing as suggested in the folklore is thus. Under the Vajra-nature Mountain there flows the pleasant stream of immortal nectar. It was here that the uninterrupted rain gave birth to the tree of long life, possessing the fruit of eight excellent flavors. Underneath this tree sits the man of long life whose immeasurable wisdom and longevity are blessed by the protector. This sage is the true manifestation of wisdom and concentration.

By living on the sacrificial pills and water offerings made by the sage, the antelopes have also attained long life. By eating the fruit of the tree of long life and drinking the nectar, the birds, too, have achieved longevity. Such things have been accomplished by the infallible law of dependent arising and the power of truth. The drawing is thought to help overcome the dangers of all life forms, of human beings, of wild animals and of all sentient beings.

—◆—

40. The Four Harmonious Friends
(*mthun pa spun bzhi*)

In the forest of Kashi, there lived a partridge, a hare, a monkey and an elephant. Speaking sincerely of their sequence of arrival in the forest, they established an order of seniority. Accordingly, this custom of animals respecting each other prevailed. Even when they travel, the

---

7   The lesser, middling and great persons are the three types of persons Buddhists believe in, based on their practices

36 *A Hundred Customs and Traditions of Tibetan People*

monkey is on top of the elephant, the hare on top of the monkey, and the partridge or grouse is on top of the hare. This noble custom serves as a deserving model for mundane existence.

Owing to this noble tradition, the region around the forest was blessed with prosperity and auspicious signs, such as timely rainfall and prosperous crops and animals. The King, ministers and masses claimed that such prosperity and happiness came out of their own merits and strength. A hermit saint with clairvoyance disagreed, and rhetorically asked by whose merits and strength did this prosperity prevail. "It is neither because of the King's merit," he said, "nor the ministers' nor the common people's, rather it is because of the merits and strength of the four animals in the forest." Everyone believed his words and they began to follow the example of the four animals. In folklore, Lord Indra, overjoyed by this way of life, with respectful and honorific words, praised the four animals:

> In the forest of austerity
> The partridge preached pure conduct
> To worldly beings.

Under this influence, Tibetans gave birth to the tradition of drawing four companions on walls, scroll paintings and wooden-boxes. Through such drawings, Tibetans convey the messages of helping each other, respecting the elders, showing care for the young and maintaining harmonious relations with each other. It also represents a deeper meaning of the fulfillment of immediate and ultimate goals of both the self and others.

—◆◆—

41. A Mongolian Leading the Tiger
(*sog po stag 'khrid*)

On the walls of affluent households there is a tradition of drawing a Mongolian leading a tiger. If someone asks why this painting is drawn, it is said that the painting dispels obstacles and hindrances;

Types of Design 37

and, it is a symbol of auspiciousness. Secondly, some believe that the drawing represents the three protectors. The physical form of the tiger represents Manjushri, the body of the man represents Avalokiteshvara, and the chain, held by the man, represents Vajrapani.

—◆:◆—

42. An Ascetic Leading an Elephant
(*a rtsa ra glang 'khrid*)

An ascetic[8] leading an elephant is one of the most popular drawings, found on the walls of Tibetans. The significance of the painting is derived from our Indian friends. In order to increase one's fortune and power, the god of wealth *(dzam bha la),* the supreme deity of the god of riches is worshipped. The physical form of *A rtsa* is the manifestation of Ganesha.[9] The elephant in the drawing is for the ascetic to ride on. Therefore, Tibetans, in order to create auspicious circumstances to gain prosperity and fortune, paint this drawing on the walls of households and monasteries.

—◆:◆—

43. Eight Auspicious Symbols
(*bkra shis rtags brgyad*)

What follows are the reasons why Tibetans regard the eight auspicious symbols with highest regard:

1 A parasol dispels the heat of ignorance.
2 The two golden fish symbolize prosperity, abandoning the faults of imperfection.

---

8 "*A rtsa ra,* a common name for Indian wandering ascetics, or sadhus, which is a distortion of the Sanskrit word acharya, meaning 'master'." (Ricard, 1997. p. 433.)

9 A Hindu god in a human form but with the head of an elephant known as the deity of wealth and prosperity

38 *A Hundred Customs and Traditions of Tibetan People*

3 The vase is a symbol of the complete fulfillment of the essence of knowledge and it is a support for virtuous merit *(rnam dkar bsod nams)*.

4 The lotus flower represents a being existing in *samsara* without attachments, purified from the defilements of body, speech and mind.

5 The white conch coiling to the right signifies the melodious sound of sublime Buddhadharma, like the melody of Lord Brahma.

6 The glorious endless knot embodies infinite knowledge and is endowed with the five wisdoms.

7 The victory banner symbolizes the victory over evil forces and heretics, and protection of all the major and minor qualities.

8 The wheel represents the dharma wheel that transfers its content – the Three Baskets of discourses and the Three Higher Trainings – within the minds of the disciples. The Mahayana *sutra* titled *The Heap of Good Fortune Sutra ('phags pa bkra shis brtsegs pa'i mdo)* states,

> Veneration to you
> With your head blessed with good fortune like a protecting parasol,
> With your body blessed with imperishable good fortune like a supreme banner of victory,
> With your speech blessed with good fortune like a right-coiled dharma conch,
> With your mind blessed with good fortune like a luminous endless knot,
> With your eyes blessed with good fortune like golden fish,
> With your tongue blessed with good fortune like an open lotus leaf,
> With your neck blessed with good fortune like a precious vase,
> With your hands blessed with good fortune like a supreme precious wheel,
> May every good fortune of these eight auspicious symbols,
> Be with us here today.
> May there be constant well-being through these auspicious symbols.

5

ARCHITECTURAL DESIGNS

44. The Colors of the Potala Palace
(*po ta lar sgron pa'i tshon gyi bstan bya*)

As anyone can see, the outer walls of the eastern and western buildings of the Potala Palace are painted white, the outer walls of the central parts are painted red, and the walls of the buildings at the eastern and lower sides of the palace are painted yellow. The three colors that decorate the external walls of the Potala Palace are not merely for appearance, but have a far deeper meaning to convey. The red signifies dominance over the three realms.[1] The white symbolizes peaceful existence on earth, and the yellow increases merit, longevity and prosperity.

The two primary colors of the Potala Palace, red and white, represent the harmonious blend of religious doctrines and secular affairs, which exist like the sun and moon. The white part of the

---

1 The three realms are: The desire realm, form realm and formless realm

40 *A Hundred Customs and Traditions of Tibetan People*

palace, which resembles a snow-capped mountain, is principally used as an administrative building, living quarters for monks and a treasure house. The red part of the palace consists of the principal halls, shrines and chapels where all the religious activities were carried out. The colors on the walls and the great craftsmanship of the building reflect the ancient system of political administration and a profound religious meaning – both a part of Tibet's unique culture.

---

45. The Four Turrets of the Potala Palace
(*rtse po ta la'i lcog bzhi*)

The four turrets (*chogs*) of the Potala Palace are the King's *chog (rgyal po lcog)*, the Great Eastern *chog (shar chen lcog)*, the Victory *chog (g.yul rgyal lcog)*, and the Tenma *chog (brtan ma lcog)*. The semi-circular King's *chog*, at the west, symbolizes the moon and the circular Great Eastern *chog* represents the mid-day sun. The simile of the sun and moon is employed to compare the co-existence of lamas and leaders to the sun and the moon, thus representing the ancient Tibetan system of unity between religious doctrine and secular affairs.

The Victory *chog* at the eastern side of the Potala Palace was built as a tribute to Gushe Tenzin Choegyal (1592-1654) and his Mongolian army, for their victory in Tibet over Tsangpa Karma Tenkyong.[2] The name of the *chog* itself suggests victory in a battlefield. The Victory *chog* is used as living quarters and no images or statues are kept inside. The Tenma *chog* is the abode or the temple of the twelve female protective deities of Tibet. The statue of the protective deity Tenma *(brtan ma)* Tashi Tsering is the most sacred statue found in this *chog*. The twelve female protective deities are among those deities subdued by Padmasambhava[3] to protect the lands of Tibet. The *chog* was built in the palace exclusively for the twelve female protective deities, and

---

2   A seventeen-century Tsangpa ruler, who was hostile to the Gelug tradition (b. 1606)

3   The lotus born tantric master who established Vajrayana Buddhism in Tibet in the 9th century, at the invitation of King Trisong Deutsen

Architectural Designs 41

is known as the shrine of deities *(srung khang)*. The shrine is regularly visited by Tibetans, who make beverage offerings.

---

46. The Circular Wall of the Potala Palace
(po ta la'i rtsigs skyor sgor mo)

When domestic and foreign tourists visit the Potala Palace, the western circular wall is used as a place to turn vehicles around. However, the youth of today have little knowledge of the origins of the circular wall and the reasons why it was built. In the early days, most of Tibet's administrative work was carried out in the Potala Palace, and government officials had to assemble for a *drung ja.*[4] At that time, horses were the only means of transportation in Tibet, and when officials attended the meetings, their servants and attendants waited, with the horses, at the western circle.

If I may cite a popular Tibetan street song, we can briefly understand the purpose of the circular walls:

> On the circular horse road,
> You, private servants, holding horses and wooly blankets tigh
> Laying your head on a Mongolian cap as a pillow,
> What did you dream of?

---

47. A Wall Made of Tamarisk Stem *(spen bad)*

Beautiful brown walls made of tamarisk stems *(spen bad)* are visible on top of monasteries, shrines and palaces. The tamarisk stalk plants are carefully selected before being arranged on top of the walls, to make ornamental tamarisk walls. The tamarisk wall is a scientific

---

4 *drung ja* is a tea offering for the sangha community organized by the government monk officials in the Potala Palace in winter and, in summer in the Norbulingka Palace

42 *A Hundred Customs and Traditions of Tibetan People*

construction material and is no doubt a unique outcome of the Tibetans' long experiences in the field of construction. Tamarisk stem is extremely light material on walls and not only reduces the weight of the structures, but also provides an easy passageway for the winds to flow through which protects walls from damage brought on by cracking or moisture. It is a magnificent and beautiful ornament.

—❖—

48. The Custom of Painting Walls
(*rtsig ngos su sa tshon sgron pa'i srol*)

The custom of painting the walls of monasteries, temples and houses in white, red, yellow and black is common in Tibet, particularly in the Tö region. Painting the sides of walls in white, red and black represents the deities of peace, increase, control, and wrath *(zhi rgyas dbang drag)* and also the three protectors.[5] White symbolizes pacification of illnesses and obstacles. Red signifies dominance over the three realms. The yellow represents longevity and prosperity. Black corresponds to the destruction of enemies and hindrances. This is similar to taking refuge in Brahma, in order to accomplish one's tasks and to overcome one's fears and is a unique ancient custom. Looking back in history, in accordance with their local conditions Tibetans took refuge in the Mongolian leading a tiger and the King Gesar, etc., respecting them as the three protectors. However, today the drawings and colors have been reduced to merely components in decorating a house, and most people are either uninterested or ignorant of the symbolic meanings.

---

5 The three protectors are: Avalokiteshvara, Manjushri and Vajrapani

6

RECREATION

49. Sports (*lus rtsal*)

Like many other nations, Tibetans have a long historical tradition of sporting events: horse racing, polo, horse riding, horse archery, wrestling, rock lifting, long jump, high jump, a game of climbing a wooden pole (*shing rsted*), sky roping (*gnam 'gro thag rtsed*),[1] tug-of-war (*glang po gnya' thag*), hammering the rocks on the chest (*pho ba rdo bshag*), skipping, swimming and so forth. I will briefly discuss a few of the sports mentioned above. Wrestling (*she ga*) is a game of strength and skill. From ancient times Tibetans loved this game and it is still played in the nomadic and farming regions during festivals like *Losar*. Youth, especially, derive great pleasure in wrestling as respite from their work.

---

[1] On the second day of the first Tibetan month, from the top of the great eastern walls of the Potala Palace, a man from Nam region would slide down on a rope tied to the monumental stone pillar (*rdo ring nang ma*) in front of the Potala Palace.

44 A Hundred Customs and Traditions of Tibetan People

Polo is one of the ancient sporting events that was played widely among the common people during the reign of early Tibetan kings. In the early eighth century, when Tibetan ministers visited the Chinese city ChangAn to invite the Chinese princess JinCheng to Tibet, the Tang emperor invited the delegates to observe the polo game at Liyuanthing. Later, a competition was organized between the Emperor's polo team and the Tibetan team.

Horse archery is a sport where a rider shoots an arrow or bullet at a target from the back of a galloping horse. This game is deeply related to military training, hunting and the traditional lifestyle of nomads. It was also a necessary military skill. During the reign of King Songtsen Gampo his powerful cavalries consistently competed in racing and horse archery. Gradually, equestrian sports found a place within Tibet's traditional sports. During festivals, horse racing is a major custom in many regions and the number of participants has grown enormously. It has become a popular sporting event of the masses.

Archery is slightly more widespread in Tibet, particularly in the Kongpo and Dromo regions. There are two types of archery; long-range archery *(rgyang mda')* and target archery *(tsha mda')*. In long-range archery, an arrow tip is fixed with a sharp pointed metal point and shot towards an object a few hundred meters away. The archery ground should be level and comfortable. The contestants are usually divided into two groups before the actual competition begins. In another kind of archery, known as *bi-shu (bi zhu)*, the arrow tip is made of hard hollowed wood and carved into an egg shape with four holes. When it is released, it creates a pleasant musical sound. So here you compete in hitting the hanging target. During an archery contest, men, women and children form a line on both sides of the contestants and sing archery songs in unison and occasionally perform folk dances. Happiness and excitement are palpable on all of their faces.

Recreation 45

50. Dice Game and other Cultural Entertainments
(*sho la sogs pa'i rig rtsed*)

Like any other country, Tibetans have a variety of traditional entertainment. I will briefly introduce a few common games like dice, Gyalpo Gyentse, Tagsa Lugsa, Sanon Namzhak, etc. Dice is one of the most widespread traditional entertainments in Tibet and is equally loved by every Tibetan. The manner in which dice is played reflects the unique characteristics of the Tibetan people. The game is not played silently; instead, participants exchange witty sayings drawing upon a variety of sources for inspiration such as history, comedy and sarcasm. Witty sayings exchanged during the dice game are not found in other games.

Generally, dice is played with two or three participants. It can also be played between teams of two people each. Depending upon the number of dots on the dice there are a variety of witty sayings which correspond to each dot. For instance, if it is *pa-ra* (a single red dot on each dice) one would say, "This *pa-ra* is Penpa Tashi and the one who is playing it is Tashi Dhondup." If the number of dots on both dices adds up to nine digits one would say, "On the nine mountains *(dgu ri ri la)* I will raise prayer flags, and I, the youth, shall shout victory to the gods." The two dices can have up to twelve dots and each number has its own specific name. For two dots it is called *pa-ra;* for three *su-ge;* for four *tsig-ge (rtsig ge);* for five *kha;* for six *lug;* for seven *ri;* for eight *sha;* for nine *gu;* for ten *chu;* for eleven *thog* and for twelve *jang (ljang).* There are also different names for each dot. If it is seven dots people have a custom of saying *ri, dhig (sdig)* or *ding.*

The game of Gyalpo Gyentse (King and Soldiers) or Tagsa Lugsa (Tiger Eating Sheep) is played on a complex path of lines where players move their pebbles in turn. This game can be played two ways: as a one-door game or a two-door game. Both of these games have small pebbles representing soldiers or sheep and slightly bigger pebbles representing the king or the tiger. The one-door game has twelve small pebbles and a slightly bigger pebble. The bigger pebble represents a

46 A Hundred Customs and Traditions of Tibetan People

king or tiger and the twelve small pebbles are for soldiers or sheep. The two-door game has sixteen small pebbles and two big pebbles. Depending upon how they move along the complex lines, a winner and loser is declared.

The other game, Sanon Namzhak, has a deep religious influence. In the past, this game was popular with monks in the monasteries and not widely played among lay people. Parallel and horizontal lines are drawn from the bottom hell to the top abode of the thirty-three deities and above the eighteen *bodhisattva* grounds. A dice is thrown and depending upon the dots, players have to move their pebbles either upward or downward. The person who reaches the top first is the winner.

Even for children, there is a custom of playing games such as bone game known as *Achug* (small bones in knee joints of goats, sheep). There are different ways to play this game; it can be played as sheep and goats, or horses and donkeys. Depending upon whether one's choice of animal is selected or not, or survives or not, a winner is declared. The game can also be played by keeping *Achug* on the wall and targeted by another *Achug* from a distance to see whether one is skilled enough to hit it.

7

MARRIAGE CUSTOMS

51. Tibetan Marriage Customs (*bod mi'i gnyen sgrig*)

Marriage customs have a definite relation to the basis of wealth and the social system. In accordance with progress in society, there have been many changes in marriage traditions. Tibetan marriage customs are practised only between a male and a female. In most cases, the bride moves into the household of the groom's family. In order to keep the family estate from being broken up, fraternal polyandry[1] and polygamy are practiced in villages and nomadic regions.

In times past, since parents took responsibility for guiding their children in the way of the world, young people rarely sought to marry based upon romantic love. Parents would first seek a bride or bridegroom of equal birth and status and consult an astrologer and see whether their birth years *(lo)* and natures *(khams)* match. If the pair

---

1 In Tibet, polyandry is when one woman marries all the brothers of a family

48 *A Hundred Customs and Traditions of Tibetan People*

is well suited for one another, then the next step is to seek divination from high lamas and deities over the future of the couple. After mutual agreement among the parents from both parties, someone from the bridegroom's family is sent with proposal-*chang (slong chang)* to further discuss the marriage dates and other details, such as an agreement or a written contract. The contract promises each will show love and respect towards parents and elders, care for the young, venerate lamas and leaders, show friendship towards their peers, and love towards those in need.

There was an ancient custom, where a young maiden was told by the family that she was being sent on a pilgrimage or to meet her relatives, but the true purpose of her journey was kept secret until she and her family had almost reached the bridegroom's house. After reaching the bridegroom's house auspicious rituals were performed.

Firstly, in the marital home auspicious substances like wheat and butter-flour, ceremonial rice, meat, butter and sacks full of grain are arranged neatly in the ceremonial room and a silk brocade or a white scarf is placed on top of them. On the mattress that the bride and bridegroom sit on, a swastika made of wheat, representing prosperity and auspiciousness, is drawn. Wild sweet potatoes *(gro ma)*, ceremonial rice, tea and *Chang* are offered on the table. The family members sit in order of seniority and the bride and bridegroom face toward the Tsang direction *(phyogs gtsang)*. A bridesmaid, usually a relative of the bride, sits beside her and serves wheat and butter-flour. The bride and bridegroom's close friends and relatives who have come to help with the ceremony stand in a row and offer ceremonial rice with wild sweet potatoes and *chang*. A group of women called *Changma*, offer *chang*, sing *gzhes chen*[2] or perform western Tibetan dance, and give a commentary on the sacred statues, pillars, large *chang* vessels and carcasses. They also deliver an oral instruction endowed with rich meaning to the bride and bridegroom:

---

2   During the wedding of an aristocrat or a high family, for auspicious reasons, men and women sing in a low long voice

Marriage Customs 49

> A mistress of the house and the holder of treasure,
> Descended not from humans but from the heavens,
> Selected among the hundreds,
> And chosen among the thousands,
> Presiding over the throne of hundreds and thousands,
> Being respectful to one's parents is the most significant,
> Who see you off with eyes full of tears,
> And welcome you with a treasure of smiles,
> Skilful you should be in ordering elder servants,
> For juniors you must teach and guide,
> Especially be kind to your male child,
> This auspicious scarf to obtain three sons in your lap,
> I offer to the princess on this auspicious occasion.

Tibetans place great importance on knowing the background and social status of a bride and bridegroom before they get married. If someone is from the occupation of a blacksmith or butcher, their birth is regarded as impure and a marriage will not be arranged for them. Furthermore, great effort is made to determine whether the person marrying into the family is related to either the father or mother. If a person is related on the paternal side, regardless of how many generations have passed, marriage is not permitted. If a person is related on the maternal side, it is made sure that he or she is not related to you by at least six generations (known as *tshigs chen gsum dang tshigs phreng gsum* meaning six joints of your hands).

—◆:◆—

52. Polyandry (*bu spun bag ma mnyam len*)

Generally, every nationality has its own unique features. From the beginning of Tibetan civilization through to the age of progress, Tibetan culture and customs have been deeply related to its economic conditions. It is the way of the world that every culture sets its own standards; however, in this age of globalization, when people from different nationalities encounter polyandry, they are surprised and

50 A Hundred Customs and Traditions of Tibetan People

look as shocked as a fool seeing God for the first time. Worse still, they may criticize the custom. If one goes with this logic then we must come to the conclusion that all the nationalities and cultures of this world should be uniform and identical; and the concept of nationality moot.

Without judging the custom, I shall now explain its origin, why it originated, and the rationale behind polyandry, without distorting the facts or exaggerating. This marriage custom emerged during the transitional period between primitive society and hierarchical society. In particular, a diverse system of production which was once exclusively dependent on a nomadic lifestyle had now become a semi-nomadic and semi-agricultural system, bringing prosperity and growth.

The main reason polyandry, which is rarely found in other societies, is common in the nomadic and agricultural regions in Tibet, is because Tibetan society relies exclusively on household production, such as dairy products. Therefore, in order to strengthen and increase the inherited family estates built through great hardships by the ancestors, and out of respect for the parents who gave you life, and to your brothers and sisters who came from the same womb, the only means to materialize one's definite wish and intention to live together and to remain united as a family, is to accept the system of polyandry.

On the contrary to this, if all the brothers of a family keep a separate wife, it is considered that the brothers dislike each other, are irreverent to their parents, lack family values and are immoral and of low status. These are the basic thoughts that led to the existence of this custom to this day. There are many things about polyandry to appreciate if one considers the alternative of a son who has developed an unethical attitude, refuses to take responsibility in life, thinks only of his own happiness, and lacks empathy towards his family.

Nevertheless, some say this system of one wife keeping many husbands is Marxist, and it is often labeled as "backward." According to traditional Tibetan healing principles, there are differences wider than the distance from the sky to the ground between a woman marrying three brothers from the same family, and three brothers from separate families. If a wife keeps three brothers as her husbands their similar nature suits her physical condition, unlike maintaining relations with men of diverse natures.

In any case, in a society where there are few old age homes, orphanages and homes for the destitute, it is undeniable that this custom of polyandry deals with a societal responsibility.

8

BON AND THE FIVE TRADITIONS OF TIBETAN BUDDHISM

53. Bon Tradition (*bon chos*)

The Bon religion is the ancient religion of Tibet. It existed before the dissemination of Buddhism in the 7th century. The Bon religion has many tenets, including Drol Bon *(brdol bon)*, Khyar Bon *('khyar bon)* and Gyur Bon *(bsgyur bon)*. Later, the great teacher Tonpa Sherab propagated the Yungdrung Bon *(g.yung drung bon)*. The earliest forms of Bon worship included offering prayers to deities and spirits and relying on exorcism to drive away evil spirits and to save the lives of sick people. Beginning with the reigns of King Nyatri and King Mutri, Bon lamas became an integral part of the court in ruling the state.

A great deal of hostility emerged between Buddhism and the Bon religion when the Tibetan kings embraced Buddhism. For instance, King Trirel (41st King of Tibet) greatly venerated Buddhism, but he had also been accused of suppressing the Bon religion and this led to

54 A Hundred Customs and Traditions of Tibetan People

his assassination by Bon ministers. His successor, King Lang Darma as per the wishes of Bon ministers, tried to uproot Buddhism from Tibet and was consequently killed by a Buddhist monk – a cataclysmic event that led to the disintegration of Tibet's royal lineage.

Later, many areas of study in the Bon religion have appeared identical to Buddhism in their philosophy, practice and meditation. *The Red Annals,*[1] authored by Kunga Dorjee, stated that the Bon has a sequence of nine vehicles. The four causal vehicles are: 1. *Shen* practice of prediction *(phywa gshen)*; 2. *Shen* of phenomenal universe *(snang gshen)*; 3. *Shen* of magic power *('phrul gshen)*; 4. *Shen* of existence *(srid gshen)*. The four resultant vehicles are: 1. Lay follower *(dge bsnyen)*; 2. Hermits *(drang song)*; 3. White quartz *(a dkar)*; 4. Bon primordial sage *(me gshen)*. The ninth one is The Vehicle of Great Distinction *(khyad par chen po'i theg pa)*.

It also says that during the reign of King Drigum Tsenpo (one of the ancient kings of Tibet), the Bon religion flourished and established a strong foundation for its tenets in Tibet. It is also stated that a complete traditional field of learning and the ways of religious activities were developed.

Followers of the Bon religion are found in places like Namling, Joda, Gojo, Markham, Kongpo Gyada, and the nine groups of Hor. *The Golden Garland of Dzogpa Rinchen* is the main text of the Bon religion and its followers seek refuge in Lord Tonpa Sherab Miwo.

---

54. Nyingma Tradition *(rnying ma)*

The tenet of Nyingma is Tibet's earliest school of Buddhism. It is often called Tibet's religion of the early propagation since it flourished some four hundred years before the later ones; hence, it is named the Old *(rnying ma)* School of Tibetan Buddhism.

---

1 *The Red Annals* is a history book, and was written in 1346

Bon and the Five Traditions of Tibetan Buddhism   55

If the teachings are looked at in terms of their meaning, there are no differences between the *sutra* of early and later propagations, but from the tantric point of view there are minor differences between the two propagations. The Nine Vehicles of Tantric Teachings of the early tantric tradition were translated into Tibetan during the reign of King Trisong Deutsen, and later taught and propagated by the Indian tantric master Padmasambhava, and held together by his disciples and others. There are nine vehicles in the Nyingma tradition: A) the Three Common Vehicles, as taught by Nirmanakaya Shakyamuni, are the hearer, solitary realizer and *bodhisattva;* B) the Three Outer Tantras,[2] as taught by Sambhogakaya Vajrasattva, are Kriya Tantra, Upa Tantra and Yoga Tantra; and C) the Three Supreme Vehicles, as taught by Dharmakaya Samantabhadra, are the Mahayoga, Anuyoga and Atiyoga.

As written in the book of tenets, *The Mirror of White Crystal (shel dkar me long)* by Thuwu Kwan, at the heart of the Nyingma tradition is the practice of Dzogchen *(rdzogs chen),* which is further classified into three sub-sections: 1) the Mind Section *(sems sde),* 2) the Space Section *(klong sde)* and 3) the Quintessential Instruction Section *(man ngag sde).* Of the Eighteen Mothers and Children of the Mind Section,[3] five originated from Vairocana and thirteen from Vilamitra. The Space Section also originated from Vilamitra.[4] The Quintessential Instruction is known as the heart essence and it originated from Vairocana. The followers of this religious tradition are called Nyingmapas.

Some of the most popular Nyingma monasteries in Tibet are Samye monastery in Lhoka, Dorjee Dak in Tsari, Mindroling in Dranang and Dzogchen, Katog and Pelyul in Kham region.

Due to a series of political and religious struggles in Tibet's history, several Nyingma monasteries were converted to the Gelug tradition. Dzogchen is the main practice of Nyingma tradition, and its followers seek refuge in Guru Padmasambhava.

---

2   Tantra is also a Sanskrit word and it refers to esoteric teachings of the Buddha
3   A lineage of Dzogchen meditation which passed down from Acarya Srimha
4   A great Indian Buddhist saint who was invited to Tibet by King Trisong Deutsen

56 A Hundred Customs and Traditions of Tibetan People

55. Kagyü Tradition (*bka' brgyud*)

The origin of the name 'Kagyü' is explained in *The Mirror of White Crystal:*

> In some of the recent documents of the Drugpa Kagyü lineage, it is written that since Marpa, Milarepa (1040-1123), Ling Repa (1128-1188) and other Kagyü masters put on white dresses, their lineage is written as Kargyü *(dkar brgyud)* – Kar *(dkar)* means 'white' in Tibetan and Gyü *(brgyud)* means 'lineage' – but the true meaning of Kagyü is someone who holds the oral transmission of the secret Kagyü teachings.

The Kagyü School was founded by Marpa Lotsawa Chöekyi Lodoe. He was born in 1012 in the village of Lhodrag Phuchukhyer. He was trained as a translator by Drogmi[5] (990-1074) and later travelled three times to India and Nepal, and received teachings directly from great *siddhas* like Naropa (active in the 11th century) and Maitripa. He also received infinite oral instructions on secret mantras, such as Hevajra, Guhyasamaja and Mahamudra. Again on his return to Tibet, he stayed at Lhodrag Drobo. His disciples included Ragton Choku Dorjee, Tsurton Wanggi Dorjee, Meton Tsonpo and Milarepa. Marpa Lotsawa attained nirvana in 1097, at the age of 86.

The followers of the Kagyü lineage are those who have received the special oral transmission of Vajradhara and practice its traditions. This tradition was introduced in Tibet. The lineage holders of great adept Khyungpo Nyaljor (978-1079) are known as Shangpa Kagyü. The lineage descended from Marpa Lotsawa is called Dagpo Kagyü. It can be further classified into four major schools: 1) Karma Kagyü, founded by the glorious first Karmapa; Knower of the Three Times; 2) Tsalpa Kagyü, founded by Shang *(zhang)* Tsalpa Tsundue – a disciple of Tsultrim Nyingpo; 3) Barom Kagyü, founded by Barom Darma Wangchuck; and 4) Phagdru Kagyü, founded by Phagdru Dorjee Gyalpo. Phagdru Kagyü has additional classifications. They include Drikung, Taklung, Drugpa, Yasang, Trophu, Shugseb, Yerpa and Mentsang.

---

5 He brought to Tibet *The Path and Result* of the Sakya tradition. His master, the great Indian *siddha* Virupa, was the founder of this lineage

Mahamudra is the main text of Kagyü practice. Some assert that the ultimate and supreme spiritual realization is called Mahamudra (the Great Seal) as the immutable bliss and, the bliss through the form having all aspects that seals it, resides as it is heard in the first moment, without increase or decrease in its actual form as long as space endures without ever transgressing it. Thus it is called seal. Since it possesses the three greats: the great abandonment, great realization and great mind, this is termed Maha; thus Mahamudra. However, some say that the meanings of the two syllables Maha and Mudra should not be explained separately. These people say Mahamudra refers to the joining of the two palms, which represents the union of means and knowledge, or the great union of clarity and emptiness *(gsal stong mnyam sbyor chen po)*.

---

56. Sakya Tradition *(sa skya)*

The main monastery of the Sakya School was founded in the chalky region of Onpo hill and is named Sakya after its site *(sa* in Tibetan means 'earth' and *kya* means 'grey'). The school of this particular tradition is also widely known as Sakya. Sachen Kunchog Gyalpo (1034-1102) introduced the Sakya tradition and built the main monastery during the Water-Ox Year (1073) of the second *rabjung.*[6] Great spiritual masters like Sachen Kunga Nyingpo (1092-1158) and the "Five Venerable Supreme Masters" further contributed towards the development of the Sakya tradition. Thus began the followers of the Sakya tradition, who practice the essence of the teachings The Path and Result *(lam 'dras).*

There are two lineages in the Sakya tradition: the Dharmic Lineage and the Family Lineage. Beginning in the Water-Ox Year of the fourth *rabjung* and because of the priest-patron relationship between Sakya Pandita (1182-1251) and the Mongol Emperor, the Sakya ruled Tibet for almost one hundred years. As suggested by the Emperor Ta Aen

---

6 *Rabjung* is a sixty year cycle of the Tibetan calendar

58 A Hundred Customs and Traditions of Tibetan People

(t'a dben) lamas, although mostly concerned with spiritual activities, should advise laypeople on acting according to spiritual practices; therefore, both the leaders and lamas engaged in political activities. Even though the Sakya tradition has many followers, Ngorchen Kunga Sangpo (b.1382) and Dzongpa Kunga Namgyal were its two most renowned upholders of tantric practice. Later, the practitioners of the secret doctrine became known as the followers of the Ngor tradition and the practitioners of the *sutra* became known as the followers of the Dzong tradition. Yagde Penchen (1299-1378) and Rongton Shakya Gyaltsen (1367-1449) are the two most renowned upholders of the *sutra* tradition. They composed numerous texts and trained a number of scholars in the five traditional fields of knowledge.

Afterwards, due to an internal conflict among Sakya followers, the lineage was divided into four groups and this led to its decline. The Path and Result is the main practice of Sakya tradition. The Sakya tradition is not only widespread in Tibet, but it is also spread widely in Mongolia.

---

57. Kadam Tradition (*bka' gdams*)

Initiated in the 11th century, the Kadam School observes a complete transmission of Buddha's oral teachings without leaving out a single word. Atisha (982-1054) founded this tradition and Dromtonpa Gyalwai Jungney (1005-1064) transmitted the lineage to his disciples. The three spiritual sons of Dromtonpa are Potowa (1031-1106), Chengawa (1101-1175) and Phuchungwa (1031-1106). They received the transmission and accepted the responsibility of upholding the Kadam tradition. Masters like Langri Thangpa (1054-1123), Sharawa (1070-1141) and Jayulwa (1075-1138) further contributed towards this tradition. The lineage disciples of the Kadam tradition are primarily classified into the scriptural traditions (*gzhung pa*), the oral transmissions (*gdams ngag*) and the pith instructions (*man ngag*). *Lamp for the Path to Enlightenment* – a text on the stages of path to enlightenment, composed by Atisha after he visited Tibet – is the main text of Kadam practice.

---

58. Gelug Tradition (*dge lugs*)

Gelug or Ganden is the name of a school derived from the Drok Riwo Ganden monastery. Je Tsongkhapa Lobsang Dakpa (1357-1419) founded Ganden monastery in 1409 and spent most of his later life living in it where he spread his tradition which is known as the Gelug tradition. There is a belief that the early Gelug tradition was called Ga-lug *(dga' lugs)*, but due to its difficulty in pronunciation it has become Gelug. Others say that the name of the tradition originates from its positive view *(lta)* and actions *(spyod pa)*. The Gelug School was founded by Je Tsongkhapa Lobsang Dakpa and held together by his spiritual sons and the disciples who follow the teachings and practices of *sutra* and *tantra*. Since the Gelug monks wear yellow hats, the Gelug tradition is often referred to as 'the Yellow Hat Tradition'.

Je Tsongkhapa Lobsang Dakpa was born in the Fire-Bird Year (1357) of the sixth *rabjung* in Domey Tsongkha region. At the age of seven he became a monk and at sixteen he left for central Tibet. As a result of ceaseless learning, contemplation, and meditation on different fields of knowledge and the Five Major Buddhist Texts, Je Tsongkhapa wrote many texts such as *Great Exposition of the Stages of the Path (lam rim chen mo)* and *Great Exposition of Tantras (sngags rim chen mo)*. He made every effort to rectify the sutric and tantric teachings. In the Earth-Ox Year (1409), he instituted the Great Prayer Festival in Lhasa *(lha sa smon lam chen mo)* and founded the Dechen Sangag Khar *(bde chen gsang sngags mkhar)* monastery. Je Tsongkhapa had many great disciples, including Gyaltsab Je (1364-1431), Khedup Je (1385-1438) and Gendun Drup (1391-1474). Je Tsongkhapa passed away in the Earth-Pig Year (1419).

60 *A Hundred Customs and Traditions of Tibetan People*

Later, the Gelug tradition flourished widely in Tibet, Mongolia and other neighboring regions. Je Tsongkhapa reformed and integrated the good qualities of other traditions into the Gelug tradition. In some regions the Gelug School is also known as 'The New Kadampa.' *The Great Treatise of the Stages to Enlightenment* is the main text of Gelug's practice.

9

Festivals

59. Losar *(lo gsar)*

The origin of Losar (Tibetan New Year) can be traced back to the reign of the ninth Tibetan King Pude Gungyal, when an old woman named Belma introduced four seasons based on the phases of the moon and the movements of the constellations. Calculating the day and the month, a whole year was believed to be completed when the apricot trees in Lhoka Yarla Shampo began to blossom with flowers after which the Spring Festival was said to begin and there is speculation that the celebration of the Losar began thereafter.

However, the celebration of the Losar differs from one region to another, according to their regional customs, traditions and agricultural seasons. For instance, in the Kongpo region Losar is celebrated on the first day of the tenth month, in the Purang region of Ngari it is celebrated in the eleventh month, and in many parts of the Ü-Tsang region it is celebrated on the first day of the twelfth month. Generally, Tibetans celebrate Losar on the first day of the first Tibetan month

62 *A Hundred Customs and Traditions of Tibetan People*

(*Hor* month). According to the oral tradition the first day of the *Hor* month is called Lama's Losar, the second, King's Losar and the third, a gathering for burning incense.

In general, the major preparations preceding Losar include the making of wheat and butter-flour, ceremonial sweet rice, green barley sprouts, *chang*, Tibetan cookies *(pin tog, mar sreg, smug thung* and *sbo lug)*, a tray full of a variety of fruits, a sheep's head decorated with a colorful butter design of the moon and the sun, tea bricks, butter kept in the dried pouch of a sheep *(mar grod ril)* and squares of buttered cheese with a swastika design done in butter. Besides that, Tibetans are busy offering food and various produce of the region, according to their wealth, on the altar or on the top of a cupboard. Moreover, people provide the best feast possible and the Five Objects of Offering[1] are decorated with the purest intentions. Also the beams, doors and windows of the houses are adorned with new awnings and curtains. New covers are also made for mattresses and cushions. Auspicious symbols like the Eight Auspicious Symbols and others are drawn with wheat flour on the black soot gathered on the kitchen walls, and on top of the fire place, a scorpion is drawn, symbolizing the female spirits of the water. On the outside in front of the entrance door, a swastika and the eight auspicious symbols are drawn in white lines. New prayer flags are made ready to hang on peaks and rooftops. In brief, provisions are made to carry out auspicious activities effectively.

On the first day of Losar, everyone gets up early in the morning and dresses themselves in new outfits and ornaments. Initially, women obtain the year's first water,[2] families make incense offerings on the rooftop, and people visit monasteries to pay homage and seek blessings. At home, to satisfy everyone's palate, they prepare Tibetan butter tea, ceremonial rice, wheat and butter-flour, *chang*, wheat porridge, boiled *chang*, Tibetan cookies and several other nutritious eatables. In an expression of their cheerful, peaceful moods, all family members greet

---

1 The Five Objects of Offerings are: 1. drinking water; 2. foot (rinsing) water; 3. flowers; 4. scented water; 5. butter lamp

2 At dawn on the Tibetan New Year, the mother of a family rushes to fetch the year's first water from water sources nearby

each other and visit their neighbors' houses and before they speak with one another they utter the auspicious words:

Wonderful that you look magnificent and healthy...
(Ae ma bag dro sku khams bzang...)

After these auspicious words are spoken, butter-flour and *chang* are offered to be flicked in the air. On the first day of Losar, people stay with their immediate family and there is no custom of visiting other people's houses as a guest. It is customary to avoid arguments, inappropriate activities and harsh words. From the second and third day onwards, people start visiting their friends and relatives. Especially in villages, Losar is celebrated in a grand manner that includes performances of the round-dance and artistic games such as throwing round stones at the target. Tibetans celebrate Losar joyfully and at great length; in many regions it is celebrated from the first day until the fifteenth day of the first month of the Tibetan calendar.

---

60. Great Miraculous Prayer Festival
(*cho 'phrul smon lam chen mo*)

The term chotrul (*cho 'phrul*) refers to the miraculous powers which arise due to the state of physical and mental pliancy. Lord Buddha, using his miraculous powers, subdued demons, heretics and other evil forces from the first day of the first month until the fifteenth day. In order to commemorate this miraculous display of power, Dharmaraja Ashoka (3rd century BC) initiated this prayer festival in India and brought prosperity, happiness and peace to every region.

The offering made during the Great Prayer Festival by Je Tsongkhapa in the first month of the seventh *rabjung* at Tsuklagkhang[3] is called the Great Prayer Festival of Lhasa. All the monks from Sera,

---

3   The main temple in Lhasa, where the statue of Jowo Shakyamuni is placed

64 A Hundred Customs and Traditions of Tibetan People

Drepung and Ganden monasteries assemble at the main temple on either the third or fourth day of the first month and begin their prayer services which continue until the twenty fifth day of the month: a total of twenty one days of elaborate offerings before the holy objects. There are three main prayer services in a day and monks are offered tea, Tibetan porridge and lambskins. Money is also distributed to them with supreme veneration, and a supplication prayer for Buddhadharma to flourish and for all sentient beings to attain happiness. After dusk, the monks who will receive the highest Buddhist doctorate degree during the prayer festival debate on the Five Major Buddhist Texts in the courtyard. Devotees travel great distances and flock to the main temple to seek blessings, and if the pilgrims offer tea and distribute some money for the Sangha community, it is considered a great fortune.

---

61. Offerings of the Fifteenth (*bco lnga mchod pa*)

The Offerings of the Fifteenth falls on the fifteenth day of the Great Miraculous Prayer Festival in the first month, which is considered one of the four major deeds of Je Tsongkhapa. It is also known as the Offering of the Fifteenth of Lhasa and is the actual day of the Great Miraculous Festival and a time to cultivate great merit. It is primarily a festival of arranging offerings and as per the lists of offerings [issued by the Government to the four great leaders (*sde dpon chen po bzhi*) and major monastic households]. Barkor Street is decorated with a series of butter offerings made of colorful butter sculptures often higher than the two- or three-storey buildings.

At the center of these sculptures, the characteristic features of Tibet's unique art and craftsmanship are displayed in colorful butter. For example, sculptures such as: Lord Shakyamuni in his palace, with the Six Ornaments and Two Supreme Ones,[4] Tsongkhapa and his chief

---

4   The Six Ornaments are Nagarjuna, Aryadeva, Asanga, Dignaga, Vasubhandu and Dharmakirti and the Two Supreme Ones are Shakyaprabha and Gunaprabha

disciples, the offering goddesses in expressions of joy and dance, the Six Signs of Long Life (see 39), the Four Harmonious Friends and Ha Shang *(hva shang)*[5] as a benefactor are displayed. And decorated in front of them are garlands of butter lamps and different kinds of offerings like constellations on the ground. During the evening, Tibetans from every corner of the country visit the main temple to see the butter sculptures. Villagers from the surrounding villages of Lhasa, like Drib and Rama Gang, spend the night singing and performing the round-dance before the butter sculptures.

---

62. Saga Dawa (*sa ga zla ba*)

On the occurrence of the *Saga (sa ga)* constellation, [as per the Tibetan lunar calendar] the full moon day of the fourth month commemorates three great occasions: the birth of Buddha, his attainment of enlightenment and his passing into *parinirvana*. Some say, Shakyamuni was born in the garden of Lumbini on the seventh day of the *Saga* month. Others believe Shakyamuni entered the mother's womb, attained enlightenment and passed into *parinirvana* on the fifteenth day of the fourth month. Thus the full moon day of the fourth month is an occasion of three festivals and highly regarded by Tibetans. As per the oral religious tradition, during the fourth month the merits and the negative deeds one commits will be exponentially increased; therefore, devoted Tibetans, as much as possible, make an effort to acquire merit by: abstaining from the consumption of meat, distributing alms to the poor, avoiding killing any life form, making offerings to the monasteries, and practicing a fast.

In old Tibet, prisoners were also released in this month and moreover, on the full moon (15th day) most of the Tibetans will refrain from eating meat. There is a Tibetan saying that even the blood-thirsty demons avoid eating meat on this day. Thousands of

---

5 A Chinese Buddhist scholar who propagated his nihilist view in Tibet

66 *A Hundred Customs and Traditions of Tibetan People*

Tibetans come out supporting the elderly and leading their children to circumambulate and visit the Potala Palace. At the same time people organize picnics in the parks and gardens like the one in Zonggyab Lukhang, etc. to celebrate this occasion.

—❖—

63. Horse Racing (*rta rgyug*)

Horse racing festivals are dearly loved by Tibetans. This tradition has a close relation to the growth in society and production in the country. Since ancient times, horses were the primary means of transport. Thus, Tibetans love keeping horses and it has become an indispensable possession for one's production and livelihood. Therefore, Tibetans hold horses in high esteem. For instance, horses are known by names, such as 'all knowing horse' *(cang shes)* and the supreme steed *(rta mchog rin po che),* and a personal deity is even referred to as a horse-headed deity *(rta mgrin).* It is clear that Tibetans consider horses as one of the most important domestic animals.

Many scholars in the past have written commentaries on horses, for instance in Namgyal Phuntsok's book, *A Clear Mirror Reflecting the Analysis of Horses:*

> From each of the five regions, gathered the nine experts on horses, each asserting their own knowledge: 'Jag and Ngu horses from the breed of Gyewo (looking upwards)/ Gyam Shing and Muchen horses from the breed of Gurpo (looking downwards)/ Dowa and Gyiling horses from the breed of Drang po (looking straight) (pp. 2,3.).[6]

From this statement, we can deduce that from the time of King Trisong Deutsen, Tibetans have classified six major breeds of horses. It is the popularity of horse racing among common people and the attitude towards horses that led to the spread of horse racing festivals in various regions of Tibet. On such a basis, horse racing festivals

---

6 The horses are generally classified into three breeds: *dgye bo, sgur po* and *drang po.* These can further be classified into twelve breeds

Festivals 67

developed in many places such as Gyaltse Damang, Kyirong Dadus (Kyirong Archery Festival), Dam Chirim *('dam spyi rim)* and the Great Changthang. During the reign of the early Tibetan Kings (who are known collectively as *btsan po*) polo was played. Thus it is clear that the custom of horse racing festivals has flourished for thousands of years in Tibet.

Equestrian sports in various regions in Tibet share similarities even though there are slight variations. In the Great Race *(rgyug chen)* the prizes are given according to the speed of the horses. Keeping in mind the advantage of a lightweight horse rider, children of ten years old participate in the race. During the actual horse race, horse riders wear clothing that reflects the artistic skills of their region and horses are adorned with riding equipment and ornaments. This is a competition to test the quality of the horses, the riding skills of the riders and the richness of their costumes. Other competitions include: Canter Competition *('gros bsdur)* where speed and gait of the horses are put to the test. An elegant and steady canter is considered to be the main feature of any horse. Besides looking for speed, the competition also awards a prize to horses with the best and most comfortable gait. A third game is called Shooting Arrows from Horseback, or Horse Archery *(zhar 'phen)* which is a competition that awards prizes to the horse rider who hits the target with their arrow or bullet— this game is a favorite among Tibetans. A fourth game is a competition of picking up white scarves while riding a horse. A few white scarves are scattered onto the track, and a horse must run at high speed while the rider simultaneously picks up as many scarves as possible. Based on the speed and the number of white scarves the rider picks up, a winner is declared.

---

64. Drugpa Tsezhi *(drug pa tshes bzhi)*

The feast of the fourth day of the sixth month is one of the major festivals celebrated annually by Tibetans. As mentioned in religious

68   *A Hundred Customs and Traditions of Tibetan People*

history texts, Lord Buddha was in silence in the *Sala* forest for forty nine days after attaining enlightenment. Brahma and Indra made an offering to him of a glittering golden wheel of a thousand spokes and a right coiled white conch shell as a means to exhort him to turn the Wheel of Dharma. On the fourth day of the sixth month, Lord Buddha decided this was the appropriate time to turn the First Wheel of Dharma, preaching the doctrine of the Four Noble Truths to his five noble disciples. From that day onwards, the followers of Lord Buddha observed this anniversary of his teaching and a custom of organizing various religious activities on this day began. Gradually, this religious ceremony became a festival of the common people. Many religious activities are carried out on this day. Tibetans not only visit monasteries and temples to pay homage and seek blessings, but there is also a custom of going out for a picnic to drink tea and *chang* and to dance and perform other recreational activities.

---

65. Universal Incense Offering
(*'dzam gling spyi bsang*)

One among the four great religious offerings, the Universal Incense Offering day was first celebrated a thousand years ago, when the Abbot Shantarakshita, the Master Padmasambhava, and the Dharma King Trisong Deutsen, successfully completed the Samye monastery. Tibetans from all levels of society widely celebrate this festival. The day is called Universal Incense Offering because people propitiate the gods, deities, *nagas,* and local spirits by making incense offerings. It is done on the occasion when Guru Padmasambhava subdued all the malevolent forces and made them the protectors of Dharma. In places like Lhasa and many other regions, this festival of incense offerings on peaks and on the banks of rivers, on the fifteenth day of the fifth Tibetan month originates from the above custom [of making incense offerings to deities, gods, *nagas,* and local spirits]. Further information

Festivals 69

regarding the nature of the smoke offering practice among common people can be found in the text of the universal incense offering in *The Epic of Ling Gesar.*[7]

66. Karma Rishi (The Bathing Festival)
(*skar ma ri shi*)

The rising of the *Rishi* Star is a bathing festival in Tibet. As per astrological texts, during the eighth Tibetan month, from the day the *Rishi* star rises, and for seven days afterwards, the water and the wind will be endowed with the eight qualities of nectar. These qualities are beneficial for medical purposes, as well as for bathing.

The occurrence of this star in autumn is the best time for bathing. The custom is to prepare a delicious meal and set out with loved ones to take a bath in hot springs to cure and protect oneself from diseases. Others also wash their mattresses and clothes and bathe in rivers and lakes nearby. This is a unique custom of the Tibetan way of life.

Common folklore suggests that if one takes a bath during the occurrence of the *Rishi* Star, it can prevent diseases. In particular, if one can visit hot springs continuously for weeks during this time, it can cure illnesses. This custom of bathing during the occurrence of the *Rishi* star is a tradition inherited from the early days.

67. Yogurt Festival or Shoton Festival
(*lha sa'i zho ston*)

The Yogurt Festival in Lhasa is an annual summer festival. At dawn on the thirtieth day of the sixth month, a giant scroll painting of Lord Buddha at the center is spread on the mountain west of Drepung

---

7 Tsetan, Kunchok. *The Epic of Ling Gesar (gling ge sar rgyal po'i sgrung 'dzam gling spyi bsang), Kan su'i mi dmangs dpe skrun khang,* 2nd ed. Ganxu People's Publishing House, 1981.

monastery. In front of this painting, operatic troupes from various regions perform a short play from their repertoires. The actual Shoton Festival begins on the first or second day of the seventh month, when operatic troupes from across Tibet present various operas and display their unique artistic skills. People from Lhasa, neighboring nomads and farmers, and Tibetans from other regions come to see the opera wearing ceremonial clothing. At the same time, they bring an abundance of food and spend days feasting in gardens with their families.

To speak briefly of the etymology of *zho ston;* there are two existing explanations. During the time of the seventh Dalai Lama, after the successful completion of Kelsang Palace at Norbulingka, a yogurt feast was arranged for all the laborers. For some, this is believed to be the origins of the festival, and its name, 'Yogurt Feast' *(zho ston)*. The other explanation claims that the name 'Yogurt Feast' originates from the custom of offering yogurt to everyone in the seventh month, since this is the time when people have an abundance of dairy products.

68. The Buddha's Descent from Heaven (*lha babs dus chen*)

Tibetans consider the twenty-second day of the ninth month as an auspicious occasion of Lord Buddha's descent to the human realm from the Tushita heaven. Tibetans therefore cultivate many virtuous deeds. It is said that after the passing away of Lord Buddha's mother, she took rebirth in Tushita. After giving sermons to his mother and other divine beings, Lord Buddha descended from Tushita on the twenty-second day of the ninth month. It is therefore a holy day and people visit monasteries to pay homage and seek blessings. They put in extra efforts toward cultivating merit by performing meritorious deeds and deviating from their usual unwholesome actions. People make offerings in the monasteries and distribute alms to the poor and beggars in accordance with their financial situation. In some regions, there is a custom of invoking oracles.

Festivals 71

69. Ganden Ngamchoe (*dga' ldan lnga mchod*)

The day commemorating the death anniversary of Je Tsongkhapa is known as Gaden Ngamchoe. Je Tsongkhapa passed into *parinirvana* on the twenty-fifth day of the tenth month of the Earth-Pig Year (1419). On this day, devoted Tibetans make offerings at the monasteries, according to their means and carry out incense offering rituals, sending thick clouds of smoke into the air. At night, the tops of monasteries and houses are lit with a series of glittering butter lamps made out of butter, oil and molten fats. Je Tsongkhapa is remembered with devotion from the depth of every Tibetan's heart. On the anniversary night, as a mark of devotion and reverence to Je Tsongkhapa, Tibetans compulsorily eat mourning porridge *(myang thug)* in remembrance of his death. Moreover, Tibetans believe that from this day onwards the actual winter season begins. In earlier days, leaders began wearing their winter dresses after this festival.

70. Ongkor Harvest Festival (*'ong skor*)

The celebration of the Summer Ongkor Festival in the farming area of Tibet can be traced back to the reign of King Pude Gungyal. One of the King's ministers, Rulekye *(Ru las skyes)*, held farming activities with high regard and during one of his initiatives to improve farming techniques, several Bon people marched all round the fields, performing rituals and saying prayers for a good harvest season. This tradition has a history of more than one thousand years and has since become a common festival for Tibetans. This festival is celebrated in a grand manner for it is a celebration of farmers seeking victory from all kinds of natural calamities and with the hope of a good harvest.

If one looks at the etymology of *Ongkor ('ong skor)*, *'ong* or *'ong kha* means field with crop on it. *kor (skor)* means walking around or circumambulating the fields and in the past when people celebrated *Ongkor* they would do so by carrying holy scriptures on their back.

72 *A Hundred Customs and Traditions of Tibetan People*

Most Tibetan farming households celebrate this festival, though the time of the festival varies. This is usually because of the diverse landscape and weather, which dictates a different time for harvesting in each region. Generally, it is celebrated for three to four days. As agricultural production increased and people's lifestyles changed, there was also a change in how this festival was celebrated. Today, Tibetans celebrate it by going out on a picnic with their loved ones, and in addition to the earlier traditions, many new competitions and artistic endeavors have been added, such as horse-racing, yak-racing, sprinting, opera and the round dance.

On the days of the *Ongkor* Festival, the family places ears of grains near the hearth deity as an offering of the fruits of the first harvest to the *nagas*. The family then prays for a good harvest after which they proceed to view cultural entertainment wearing ceremonial attire and carrying *chang* and other foods. They enjoy cultural entertainment as well as inviting their loved ones and relatives to their house as guests.

---

71. Rooftop Smoke Offerings (*thog gsol*)

The Rooftop Smoke Offerings is an auspicious day selected during Losar, according to astrological texts. As one of the major Losar activities, people climb onto their roofs in the morning to replace the old prayer flags with new ones and these are known as offerings to the divine spirits. After the old prayer flags are replaced with the new ones, the new flags are offered with smoke offering rituals and marked with butter-flour. In eight main and intermediate directions, butter-flour is sprinkled in the air while shouting in unison and repeating the phrase, "Victory to the gods" *(lha rgyal lo),* and at the same time entrusting the divine spirits to help in achieving prosperity in work and preventing obstacles in the New Year. Loved ones and their neighbors gather together to drink tea and *chang,* and to sing and dance traditional dances after the invocation and offerings to the divine spirits. However, in places like Lhasa, the celebration takes place

Festivals 73

on rooftops which are decorated with carpets and tables, a wooden tray of butter-flour, an abundance of tea, *chang* and snacks. In the morning the neighbors dress in their best costumes and ornaments and gather on the rooftop to perform the smoke offering ritual. Then people sit in order of seniority and engage in joyful activities such as drinking tea, *chang*, singing, playing games and engaging in conversation.

The occasion of Rooftop Smoke Offerings is not merely an activity of putting up new flags and making offerings to the divine spirits. It is also an occasion to deepen one's relations with the neighborhood, and a means to emphasize the importance of mutual relationships. It also conveys a powerful message to overcome all obstacles between you and your neighbors by stepping forward to help and show concern for one another.

10
THINGS TO AVOID

72. The Purpose of Circumambulating Clockwise rather than Counterclockwise
(nang skor las phyi skor la 'dzem dgos don)

The reason Tibetans avoid circumambulating counterclockwise is in harmony with walking to the right side while turning, which is one of the eighty minor marks of a Buddha, "To proceed towards the direction in accordance with the path of Dharma is the right turning circle of the eighty minor marks." The followers of Lord Buddha should pay attention to the distinction between right and left, clockwise and counterclockwise. The right side is considered superior and clockwise, while the left is considered inferior and counterclockwise. Even with regard to rows, the people sitting on the right side of a row are considered of higher rank. Thus, devotees developed a custom of circumambulating clockwise and avoiding counterclockwise, they consider it unwholesome to circumambulate counterclockwise. From a religious point of view, this is often used as a reason to distinguish Buddhists from non-Buddhists.

76 *A Hundred Customs and Traditions of Tibetan People*

73. What to Avoid during Obstacle Years
(*kag dus kyi 'dzem bya*)

Tibetans take great care to avoid a number of activities when they reach certain obstacle years. Though the details of actions to be avoided during an obstacle year can be found in astrological texts, a few of the main activities Tibetans avoid are: house construction, renovation, other construction-related works and visiting people who are affected with chronic illnesses. The number of animals to be killed at the end of the obstacle year must be reduced and children's marriages should not be arranged. The obstacle year for men is thirty-seven, for women it is forty-nine, and for children it is thirteen. When people reach these ages, they remain careful and avoid the above activities. It is believed that if the obstacle year of thirteen went off smoothly, then all other obstacle years will be relatively peaceful.

The main method of overcoming obstructions is done through a ceremony called 'changing appearances' *(lus bsgyur)*, such as wearing yellow clothes with a sun, moon and swastika pattern. There are also different prayers that can be recited. A common belief is that if a dog jumps up at you during the obstacle year of thirteen, then the following obstacle years will be peaceful, but if a dog does not jump at you, then you must hold a dead dog by its tail and make three clockwise circles and three counterclockwise circles in order to get rid of all other obstacles.

---

74. Things to Avoid Related to Polite Behavior
(*gus zhabs dang 'brel b'i 'dzem bya*)

Tibetans have a good custom of showing respect towards elders and caring for the young. For instance, while talking to a senior person, one must use honorific terms. While saying their names, the suffix *'lags'* must be attached after the name to show respect and regard. There is no custom of calling the names directly.

Pushing to make your way through a crowd while on the roads, stretching out one's legs and hands rather than sitting cross-legged in

Things to Avoid 77

your house, farting in public, passing a broom directly into someone's hand, sweeping immediately after a person leaves on a journey, spitting behind someone's back and, women shaking their aprons in public are behaviors and modes of conduct that are considered highly disparaging and can be evil omens to others. Therefore, they should be avoided.

In addition, mendicants, the elderly and the disabled are given assistance and generous gifts. It is considered low and immoral to belittle and reprimand less fortunate people.

---

75. What to Avoid between Relatives
(*spun mched bar gyi 'dzem bya*)

In Tibetan customs and traditions, a sense of decency should be maintained between male and female relatives: between fathers and daughters, brothers and sisters, uncles and nieces, aunts and nephews. Obscene talk should be avoided and relatives should never watch obscene shows together. For instance, if it is necessary to discuss marriage, a boy will talk to his father while a daughter will talk to her mother – daughters do not talk about marriage with their fathers nor do sons discuss marriage with their mothers.

These practices are avoided because marriage and all other worldly activities related to attachment and craving are considered to be associated with unethical behavior. Even a conversation on these matters is considered an unwholesome deed.

---

76. Things to Avoid after Someone's Death
(*mi shi byung rjes kyi 'dzem bya*)

Tibetans avoid making physical contact with a dead body until it has received the 'transference of consciousness' ceremony (*'pho wa*) from a lama. The family and the relatives avoid plaiting or braiding their hair and washing their faces until the period of mourning has passed.

78 *A Hundred Customs and Traditions of Tibetan People*

They also avoid wearing new clothes, bringing down the rooftop flags, singing songs, dancing and playing games. Even the neighbors and loved ones observe these customs in order to show their grief. Furthermore, during the funeral procession, glancing back and, when the *chang* of sadness *(sdug chang)* is offered, sprinkling of it in the air (as a sign of auspiciousness) should be specially avoided. Other actions to abstain from include: taking rests on the way of the procession, visiting the houses of the deceased after the corpse has been given to the birds and taking leftover salt and food to one's house.

---

77. Food and Drinks Which Need to be Avoided
(*bza' 'thung thad kyi 'dzem bya*)

Tibetans avoid many foods. The five meats that should be avoided unequivocally are of human, elephant, dog, vulture and horse. It is only acceptable to eat animals that have lower teeth and split hooves, such as yak, *dri,* ox, sheep, goat and so forth. Domestic animals with lower and upper teeth and those with closed hoofs, such as mules and donkeys, are avoided completely as are clawed carnivorous animals like tigers, leopards, bears and wolves. Among birds, except a few like swans and cranes, there is no custom of eating birds like sparrows and pigeons. Similarly, all the clawed animals like mice are not eaten.

Pertaining to aquatic animals, only fish is eaten and there is no custom of eating frogs, turtles or lobsters. Even though people eat yak, *dri,* goat and mutton, they do not eat them on the day they were slaughtered. On holy and auspicious days, devout followers of Lord Buddha eat only *dkar skyong[1]* and keep themselves away from meat.

On festival days, during auspicious gatherings and if one is a guest, it is considered highly inauspicious if someone serves you a mug that has a chip in it or is slightly cracked.

---

1 Food not mixed with meat, bones, fats or blood

78. Things to Avoid during Losar
(*lo gsar skabs kyi 'dzem bya*)

On the first day of Losar, people pay great attention to initiating only auspicious actions and abstaining from unwholesome conversations and inauspicious actions, so that prosperity, good luck and the spontaneous fulfillment of one's wishes can be achieved in the new year. On the first day of Losar, in order to achieve prosperity, people avoid sweeping their houses, indulging in disputes, passing inappropriate remarks, criticizing others, and borrowing and lending food or objects from neighboring households. They are careful not to break cups, plates and utensils.

If any of the above happens, it is considered a bad omen/ premonition. Some rely on particular methods, like reading scriptures or receiving a blessing from a high lama, to overcome such obstacles, while others halt their business activities and engage only in activities related to happiness and joy. There is a saying, "Fold your joints on the first and second day of Losar". It means that people should sit back and relax.

---

79. What to Avoid near Monasteries
(*dgon 'gram gyi 'dzem bya*)

In an area close to a monastery, temple or hermitage, people should generally refrain from chopping trees, screaming, singing loudly, hunting or fishing. In particular, people should refrain from inflicting any kind of harm on wild animals and birds. Visiting monasteries and touching holy statues inside monasteries after eating garlic or smoking are strictly prohibited.

---

80 *A Hundred Customs and Traditions of Tibetan People*

80. What to Avoid in the Company of Sick People
(*nad pa'i mdun gyi 'dzem bya*)

If a house has a sick person or a pregnant woman delivering a baby, there is a custom of denying entry to outsiders in order to ward off obstacles and harm. This custom varies from region to region. In some regions, if there is a sick person in a home, various numbers of cairns are made – based on the seriousness of the disease – to warn visitors. If the illness is not that serious, a single pile of stones is erected. Two piles of stones are erected for a quite serious disease and three for a very serious disease. In some regions, instead of cairns, people use smoking ash while others tie a piece of red cloth to their door frame. Though the customs differ, they are all intended to inform outsiders to avoid entering the house.

---

81. What to Avoid near the Cooking Area
(*me thab sogs kyi 'dzem bya*)

Tibetans are very cautious to not let things that give off a bad smell melt on their stoves/hearths. For instance, the burning of flesh, bones and old clothes should be avoided. Besides this, placing one's feet on the stove/hearth and stepping over it should be avoided. Keeping cups and other vessels facing down, whistling in your home and carrying empty baskets while visiting the houses of others should also be avoided.

---

82. What to Avoid in Fields and on Mountain Peaks
(*'ong kha dang ri khar 'dzem dgos pa'i skor*)

During summer, there are many things that Tibetans should avoid while walking in fields. Women should not walk in fields without wearing aprons, head ornaments, hats or scarves and they must not

Things to Avoid 81

let their black hair hang loose. Carrying red meat and taking a funeral procession through fields is strictly prohibited. People should also avoid shouting and screaming in fields and on top of mountains. If someone does this, people believe that it will upset the local deities and spirits and fields could be destroyed by hailstones and lightening.

—◆—

83. Avoidance of Killing (*srog gcod la 'dzem don*)

The majority of Tibetans follow Buddhadharma. Being a follower of Lord Buddha, Tibetans believe in past and future lives, and in the law of karma. Taking someone's life is considered the most serious negative action and, among objects to be abandoned, the act of killing should be the most important. A few spiritual teachers have eaten yak's meat and mutton, but they only eat the meat with three-fold purity,[2] and are not allowed to slaughter animals themselves.

—◆—

84. Day of the Conjunction of Nine Evils (*ngan pa dgu 'dzoms*)

On the sixth night and the seventh day of the eleventh Tibetan month, the demigod Nyima Nagchen meets the nine evil spirits owning the earth. This period is considered highly inauspicious. The day following this meeting is considered auspicious and is called the Day of Conjunction of Ten Auspiciousness. In the oral tradition of Tibet, there is a saying that, "If you are the Day of Conjunction of Nine Evils, I am the Day of Conjunction of Ten Auspiciousness."

Furthermore, on the Day of the Conjunction of Nine Evils, astrological texts recommend "avoiding food that is the subject of

---

2 Meat with three-fold purity is: 1) It must be obtained without suspicion, 2) the animal must not be killed specifically for you, or raised specifically for you, and 3) You must not see the animal being slaughtered

82 *A Hundred Customs and Traditions of Tibetan People*

dispute, galloping in northern directions, and speaking of the Victor's words." On this day people avoid work. It is a day of relaxation and some people invite their loved ones for a gathering.

The festival has no direct relation to the popular story "The Conjunction of Nine Bad Omens" in the biography *The Wish-fulfilling Tree* depicting the Deeds of Lord Buddha.

11

Lifestyle

85. Guthuk *(dgu thug)*

On the twenty-ninth day of the last month of the Tibetan calendar, an effigy ritual is performed throughout the country with the purpose of purging obstacles and mischance of the past year, and expunging evil spirits from the house. *Guthuk* (a special Tibetan gruel) is prepared with nine different kinds of ingredients. Leaving aside all other work, detailed work of the day includes thorough cleaning up of every room – especially the year-long soot gathered on the kitchen wall.

In the evening, as the name of the feast suggests, *guthug* is prepared. Unlike the usual Tibetan gruel, in order to symbolize individuals' positive and negative characteristics and ways of thinking, figures like the sun and moon made of dough are wrapped in slightly bigger dough of uniform sizes, which will be served randomly with the gruel. If someone finds the sun or the moon, then it symbolizes dignity and fame; the shape of a small rectangular carpet symbolizes comfortable and easy times ahead; white wool symbolizes a calm and good-natured

84 *A Hundred Customs and Traditions of Tibetan People*

person; porcelain symbolizes skill at locating food and avoiding work. Another feature that makes *guthug* unique from other feasts is the mixture of nine different kinds of ingredients including meat, radishes and cheese.

Furthermore, in a broken clay vessel or on a metal sheet, an effigy of a person as a ransom is surrounded by used tea leaves, leftover grains from the *chang*, leftover food, small pieces of trash, and dirt from the house. In both their hands, the family members take a piece of dough made of barley flour and roll it down from head to toe murmuring, "You the effigy, take away all the disharmonious elements: sicknesses of the body, unsatisfactory states of mind, and the 424 different types of diseases, that come along in a year, 12 months and 360 days, and go beyond the big ocean." They then spit on the dough and squeeze it in each hand to leave a handprint on it, and place it around the effigy. When it becomes dark outside, elders and children in the family enter every room shouting "come out" while they hold a stick with a flame and banish the effigy at a crossroad.

---

86. Tsampa *(rtsam pa)*: A Roasted Barley Flour

Tsampa is ground flour made of washed and roasted barley or wheat. Tsampa can be made from barley, bean, rice, and other roasted grains. In roasted barley flour there are low-quality *tsampa*, medium-quality *tsampa*, offering *tsampa*, and finely ground *tsampa*. The finely ground *tsampa* is high quality roasted barley flour, finely grounded, and made through the process of careful cleaning and skinning of the roasted barley. The other types of *tsampa* are not so popular and slightly coarse in nature.

Roasted bean flour is another high-quality *tsampa* made of finely ground beans with the skin removed. Generally, there are two kinds of bean flour: one with skin and the other without.

An important feature of *tsampa* is that it is convenient to eat and easily consumed at home or on the road. As per the individual's taste, one can knead *tsampa* with tea, *chang* or whey and eat it with vegetables. If one does not have this facility one can still eat it with water. *Tsampa* can also be eaten dry or made into delicious buttery balls *(mar zan)* of cheese, sugar, butter or oil. It can also be prepared as *tsampa* porridge, hot *chang,* or rancid cheese porridge. It can be mixed with tea or *chang* to make a thick or light porridge. People can further add yeast to the barley dough *(pag)*, and make *chang* lumps *(zan chang)* in elongated and round figures and then dry them to eat like cookies that satiate hunger and thirst.

Tsampa is usually made of barley, which has a unique feature unlike any other grains: the components of barley are healthy for the human body and can cure diseases. The Tibetan staple food *tsampa* is endowed with this excellent natural quality – a fact acknowledged long ago in Tibetan medicine. From the modern medical point of view, *tsampa* is endowed with the qualities to cure cardiac diseases.

—◆:◆—

87. Chang *(bod chang)*

The Tibetan custom of drinking *chang* has a long tradition. The book *The Treatise of Tea and Chang Goddesses* gives evidence of this:

> During the inauguration of the Yumbu *(yum bu lha khang)* Palace of Nyatri Tsenpo, and on many other occasions, the beverage of Deden Dutsi *(chang)* was taken by successive Religious Kings. Moreover, the famous special bowl *('khrung snod)* of the most incomparable King Songtsen is still preserved as a sacred object in the Great Palace. Thus, it is implied that there is a long history since the spread of this custom of drinking *chang.*

Tibetans, in accordance with the climate of their regions, the production level of that time, and their standards of living, have all contributed towards the development of this beverage called *chang.*

As known to everyone, the food and beverages of Tibetan people are endowed with special qualities that allow the food and drink to be eaten both inside and outside the house. For instance, in the case

86 *A Hundred Customs and Traditions of Tibetan People*

of *chang*, it can quench the thirst and also be used as soup in making barley dough. In cold weather, one can boil and drink it hot. Therefore, we can say, *chang* is an indispensable drink in Tibetans' lives. In the celebration of auspicious occasions and in moments of obstacles and hindrances, *chang* is a necessary item. There is a saying in Tibet:

> *Chang* is a happy companion in times of happiness
> A sorrowful companion in times of sorrow
> Happiness and sorrow in whatever way they come
> *Chang* will keep you company.

At dawn on the first day of Losar, the first drink should be boiled *chang*. After the feast, at any gatherings, the guests are served with bowls of *chang*. In order to symbolize sincerity, guests at home are served three bowls of *chang*. Even while receiving or seeing off relatives and guests, farewell-*chang (skyel chang)* and welcome-*chang (bsu chang)* are drunk. A wedding ceremony in Tibetan is called '*chang sa*' for it is a 'gathering of drinking *chang*'. The reason for saying that *chang* is an indispensable drink in Tibetans' lives is as depicted in the book of *The Treatise of Tea and Chang Goddesses:*

> *Chang* is the strength of the voice of the joyous singers,
> The footsteps when one dances happily,
> The consolation when one weeps in sorrow,
> The key to open speech,
> The brain for the thousand-headed wise man,
> The encouragement to subdue the enemy
> And the escort to escape through narrow passages.

❖

88. Ceremonial Rice *(gro ma 'bras sil)*

Tibetans eat ceremonial rice as the first food item on the first day of Losar. Ceremonial rice is also served at wedding ceremonies and on other auspicious occasions. Ceremonial rice is an auspicious food symbolizing prosperity and good fortune.

Rice is the fairest among the grains and its white color is a symbol of auspiciousness and prosperity. In the lists of enumerations of names, rice is known as "the pearl of conch" and "the endless knots" and these are two of the eight auspicious symbols and the foremost symbols of auspiciousness.

Secondly, in the Tibetan mindset, "fruit", [which in Tibetan is the same word for rice] is considered precious, and to ripen to fruition is often compared to the fulfillment of one's future plan. For instance, when elderly people pass away, it is said that they have "ripened to fruition". Thirdly, there is a custom of mixing ingredients like small dried wild sweet potatoes *(gro ma)* and raisins in ceremonial rice. Small dried wild sweet potatoes suggest auspiciousness and raisins are considered superior among the fruits. Finally, the lists of enumerations of names also refer to raisins as "taste of honey" *(sbrang gi ro)* and "tasty" *(ro ldan)* and this implies spontaneous fulfillment of one's wishes like the sweetness of honey.

---

89. Tea *(gsol ja)*

Tibetans love drinking tea and it is an indispensable beverage in the Tibetan lifestyle. It is customary to drink tea every morning and guests at home are never left unserved and are always greeted with tea. Different kinds of Tibetan tea are butter tea, black tea, and sweet tea.

In the Ü-Tsang region there is a custom of making *jakhu (ja khu)*. *Jakhu* is made by adding a small quantity of tea and *bul thog* (a kind of soda obtained from a northern district in Tibet) in water and boiling it for a long time. The strong black tea *(nying khu)* is then stored in a clean vessel. A quick and convenient way to make tea is by adding a small quantity of strong black tea into boiling water with salt and butter. It is then churned to enhance the flavor. However, in the Kham region there is no custom of adding black tea, and the teas are made and drunk instantly.

88 *A Hundred Customs and Traditions of Tibetan People*

In the Amdo region, people prefer drinking black tea, and they do not have a custom of drinking butter tea. In cities and towns, people prefer drinking sweet tea – there are plenty of sweet tea stalls. If people are not in a hurry and have time, they love to visit tea stalls and talk about anything and everything. This popular tradition of drinking tea in Tibet is related to the environmental needs of the high altitude and the dryness of the region.

In Tibet, there is a folktale about the origin of tea that dates back to the reign of King Düsong Mangpo. One day, the King was gripped by a severe sickness and there was no one with capable knowledge of the practice of medicine. He decided to dwell in meditation. At one point he witnessed, at the corner of a building, a previously unseen beautiful bird singing melodiously with a leaf on a twig in its mouth. The King paid little attention to it. However, it became a recurrent event for several days, and the King began to intently study the twig. This twig was not familiar to the King and he was uncertain of it, but decided to put one end of the stick into his mouth to taste it and his thirst was instantly quenched. Having considered it the supreme beverage, the King ordered:

> All you ministers and commoners – Listen closely!
> In my time of sickness; to drink and eat others I had no desire,
> This twig brought by the bird is the supreme drink that heals the body,
> A medicine for illness; therefore those who feel close to me,
> Should search for this plant,
> A big reward will be offered.

The ministers and the common people searched the entire land of upper and lower Tibet to find this plant but could not. However, one minister with pure dedication to the King wandered across Tibet. Finally, he reached a thick bamboo forest in China thinking he would definitely find the tree there. He walked towards the forest, but there was a large body of water preventing him from getting to it. He was certain to find the particular wood in this forest and kept thinking of his King's image. Suddenly, he saw a fish moving in the water and realized that the water was not deep though it appeared wide. Afterwards he swam across the water and reached the forest. He felt relieved to find the same wood brought by the bird and thought this plant would certainly heal the King's body. With great delight, he tried carrying the log on his back, but he had second thoughts. He believed this tree would certainly heal the King's sickness, but the road was too long. He wished for a friend or a load-carrying animal to help him. While he was deep in thought, a female deer came near him, and he felt that the deer would be able to carry the load. The minister prepared the load with one end of the log on the deer and the other on his back. The deer accompanied him for days and months until the King's palace became visible in the distance. Upon his return, the minister presented the logs to the King, and pleased by the minister's work, the King greatly honored him with a reward for the tea which had improved the King's health. If the saying, a custom of drinking tea begins from the reign of King Düsong Mangpo is reliable, then the term *ja* (tea) is a name ascribed on reason. But, some may ask why *ja* (tea) is not written as *bya* in Tibetan.[1] This is primarily intended to avoid confusing *ja* (tea) with *bya* (bird).

90. Water Offering *(chu phud)*

At dawn on the first day of the Losar, when the first cock crows, the housewife of the family sets out to fetch the year's first bucket of water *(chu phud)* before any other families do. She carries an empty bucket on her back and *chang*, butter-flour, and incense in her hand. After reaching the water source, she offers prayers and makes a wish to the female water spirit by burning incense and offering *chang* and tea.

After the offerings, the housewife fetches the water, and returns home without glancing behind her. There is a traditional belief that if the housewife glances behind then she might lose the good luck of

---

1 *Bya* and *ja* are pronounced the same

90 *A Hundred Customs and Traditions of Tibetan People*

her New Year's bucket of water. Upon reaching home, water offerings are made [in the form of seven water bowls to the Three Jewels]; the leftover water is poured into a large copper vessel. Boiled *chang* porridge is brewed with the remaining water and serves the family members as a mark that begins the auspicious Tibetan New Year.

12

Death Ceremonies and Funeral Rites

91. The Disposal of Dead Bodies
(*phung po dur 'jug*)

Tibetans have five methods of disposing of dead bodies: 1) raising reliquary; 2) cremation; 3) casting into the waters (lakes and streams); 4) ground burial; and 5) sky burial. I shall briefly discuss the first four. Constructions of reliquaries *(mchod rten)* are done after the passing away of highly incarnate lamas; mainly the case of successive Dalai Lamas, Panchen Lamas and great spiritual lamas. The bodies of such holy beings are embalmed and wrapped by smooth clothes and placed in reliquaries made of gold and silver, and venerated as objects of reverence. In the case of other lamas, *trulkus* and great persons, their bodies are cremated. For common people, if the conditions are not favorable to give the body away to the birds, then it is cast into rivers as a form of offering to fish. Others such as dead criminals (charged with murders and thievery), and people who die of epidemic diseases and

92 A Hundred Customs and Traditions of Tibetan People

pestilence are buried beneath the ground. This is considered the worst method of disposing of dead bodies. The dead body of a child is kept inside a clay pot and buried in the cleft of rocks on a mountain.

---

92. Sky Burial (*phung po bya gtor*)

In most regions of Tibet, there is a custom of offering dead bodies to vultures. This custom has existed in Tibet for more than nine hundred years. It is definitely a tradition that has gradually flourished after the dissemination of Buddhism in Tibet. Prior to this – from the head of the state King to the poorest of citizens – people were buried in tombs and there was no custom of giving bodies to the birds. The flourishing of sky burials is based on the episode in the *Jataka Tales*[1] of Buddha giving his body to the tigress *(stag mo lus sbyin)*. Just like the *Jataka Tales*, it is a genuine effort from Tibetans to practice generosity by giving away their bodies (of flesh and blood) by feeding vultures and fish.

According to religious history, during the early twelfth century, Phadampa Sangye[2] founded Shijey *(zhi byed)* tradition in Tibet, which led to the beginning of the practice of Transforming the Aggregates into a Food Offering *(phung po gzan bskyur)* of Machig Labdrön[3] and the *Chö* tradition. And due to the influence of the practice of Transforming the Aggregates into a Food Offering Tibetans began to give away their dead bodies to animals. Tibetans hope to attain a higher status in the next life as a result of practicing this kind of generosities. Folklore suggests some reasons why dead bodies are offered to vultures. Vultures are considered as the protector of the charnel grounds, and it is believed that among the bird species, vultures are considered as the

---

1 The story of the previous lives of Lord Buddha

2 Phadampa Sangye was an Indian master who visited Tibet five times and introduced the Pacification of Suffering teachings *(zhi byed)* to Tibet. He died in 1117.

3 Machig Labdrön (1103-1201) was a great female *siddha;* who was a principal disciple of Phadampa Sangye

king of birds who soar to great heights, and if the bodies are offered to them, people can expect a higher rebirth.

—◆—

93. Funeral Rites ('das mchod)

Tibetans observe funeral rites and a death anniversary in order to express their gratitude, commemorate the great works of the deceased and show their solidarity. In accordance with religious tradition, it is considered the responsibility of the family to purify the evil deeds and obscurations accumulated by the deceased.

If someone passes away, relatives, loved ones and neighbors pay a visit to the mourning family to show solidarity and condolence with grief-*chang*, tea and donations for butter lamps. After the funeral procession is completed, weekly virtuous actions[4] are performed for the deceased person [for seven weeks]. Funeral rites such as offerings to the Three Jewels and giving gifts to the needy are carried out. The first and the fourth 'weekly virtuous acts' are considered highly significant and during each of these weeks, loved ones, relatives and neighbors visit the family of the deceased with a white scarf, tea, *chang* and donations for butter lamp offerings. The family is expected to express grief and sorrow.

Many rituals are performed on the seventh 'weekly virtuous act'. This is known as *shegu (zhe dgu)*, or the 49th day since the person passed away. Friends, loved ones, relatives and neighbors all visit the family and offer tea, *chang* and donations for butter lamp offerings. After the completion of the 49th day, the family of the deceased gradually returns to their normal daily life. The family observes a religious ceremony called the annual ritual *(lo mchod)* exactly one year after the death. At this time, the family invites their relatives, loved ones, friends and neighbors, and offers a lunch as a symbol of expressing gratitude for the help they gave in times of misery. It also formally ends the family's grief.

---

4   Virtuous practices for the accumulation of merit

13

KINDS OF DECORATION

94. A Mirror of Twelve Cycle Years
(lo 'khor me long)

Deeply ingrained in the Tibetan mindset is the religious belief that evil spirits and demons might inflict harm and obstacles. Therefore, Tibetans have developed different measures to ward off these evils and obstacles. One such measure, according to Chinese astrology is to tie a brass plate *(me long)* to your waist drawn with *parkha (par kha)*,[1] *mewa (rme ba)*,[2]

---

[1] Parkha or "The Eight Trigrams" are arranged in a circle around the *mewa* within the astrological charts. These eight *parkhas* move around the chart from year to year. The eight parkha are called: 1. Suli; 2. Khon; 3. Dva; 4. Khen; 5. Kham; 6. Gin; 7. Zin; 8. Zon. These relate respectively to: 1. Fire; 2. Earth; 3. Pond; 4. Heaven; 5. Water; 6. Mountain; 7. Thunderbolt Iron; and 8. Wind.

[2] Nine *mewas* are figures arranged in a magic square. The figures in the magic square, whether added diagonally, horizontally, or vertically, always give a sum of 15. These figures are symbolical of the element of metal, water, wood, earth, and fire.

96 *A Hundred Customs and Traditions of Tibetan People*

the twelve-year cycle wheels and a *zipar (rdzi par).*[3] There is a belief that a mirror can ward off inauspicious directions such as *bumtong*, and it can also ward off inauspicious hours during the rise of malignant stars and block any harm from *nagas*, evil spirits and other earth-owning spirits *(sa bdag).* This custom of tying a mirror to the waist originated from such beliefs. However, I have not seen any reliable documents, so I am offering this write-up for further research.

---

95. Aprons (*dpang gdan*)

If I may speak on how this custom of wearing attractive and colorful aprons began and how it changed over time. Aprons that we see Tibetan women wearing today are the result of continual improvement. This custom of wearing an apron may have originated from the needs of the lifestyle and climate of the region. Initially, women wore an apron to hold a baby in their laps. Secondly, Tibetan women are extremely hardworking and very skillful in managing domestic chores, therefore when they go outside their houses, they have a habit of using their aprons as a kind of convenient basket to keep all the firewood and fodder grass lying on their way. Thirdly, with the apron tied at the front, it helps keep the body warm by blocking the cold wind.

As society has progressed, so too has the quality of living and this is reflected in the continued improvement of the color and quality of the aprons, that were initially intended for utilitarian purposes and have now become an exquisite traditional outfit. Presently, aprons worn by Tibetan women are merely beautiful traditional attires with a vast variety of colors and a great emphasis on its quality. There are different varieties of aprons made with heavy woolen cloth, fine serge and silk. In order to make the apron more beautiful people use *druden*

---

3   Zipar or Kirtimukha is a common motif found in ancient Indian temples and in Tibet. The face of Kirtimukha is usually drawn with a protruding tongue, bulging eyes and festoons of pearls hanging from its mouth.

(gru gdan; silk brocades at the edges of the apron) and *kinkhab (kin khab;* triangular patches that attach the waist strap to the apron). The colorful apron has become a unique, traditional Tibetan woman's dress. Each region has its own way of tying the apron. For instance, the women in the Tö region tie the apron at both the front and the back. The aprons tied at the back are decorated with silver and other ornaments, while in central Tibet, women never put on an apron until they are married.

---

96. Fur Ornamentation for Clothing
(gzigs lpags kyi mtha' rgyan)

The Tibetans' style of embroidering tiger and leopard skins over the edge of their traditional dress is not merely a creative ornamentation; it has its own history of origin and purpose. During the reign of the early Tibetan Kings, a tiger skin was given as a reward for brave acts on the battlefield. Among the six conditions,[4] a tiger skin signifies courage and a hat made of fox skin signifies cowardice. These objects are unique symbols of the titles and positions in ancient Tibet. With political and social changes, this gradually turned into an ornamental design in the common people's dress. A traditional Tibetan dress *(chupa)* with ornamental designs of tiger and leopard skins on the collar and the edges is considered superior to other plain *chupas.*

The scriptural texts say that a tiger skin worn by warrior spirits *(dgra lha)* and powerful local deities symbolizes the realization of emptiness; however, in reality, it has a deep association with an old Tibetan custom of rewarding bravery with a tiger skin.

---

4   The six conditions are the conditions of courage, coward, virtue, hero, low caste and evil.

14

OTHER CUSTOMS

97. Head Letters (*yig mgo 'bri srol*)

The Tibetan script, unlike the scripts of other nationalities has a unique characteristic of writing head letters (*yig mgo*). This section was written based on the combined research of scholars and interviews with them as documents were not found that explain the purpose and history of writing head letters. Essentially, head letters are written because they symbolize auspiciousness. As in every work and object, Tibetans believe there is a head (beginning) and tail (end), and are fond of symbols that signify auspiciousness. If one carefully analyzes the shape of head letters and stacked-head letters, one finds the figures of the sun and the moon. In the Tibetan mindset, the sun and the moon are viewed as symbols of changelessness and it can be said that the head letters are written as an auspicious sign that the Tibetan language will exist until the sun and the moon cease to glow.

Generally, a head letter is written in most genres of text, but in the case of a donation envelope for a deceased person, there is no custom of writing a head letter.

98. Yokes (*gnya' btsug*)

In the farming regions of Tibet, when the farmers plow their fields, as an ornament they tie prayer flags to the yoke and a red cloth on the tail of the cattle. There is a folktale that begins with an old man plowing his field with his yaks when suddenly a giant bird appears. The bird, which came from the upper part of the valley, almost created an eclipse and shook the entire place with one flap of its wing. The bird grasped the old man, the yak and the plowshare in its claws, and disappeared into the sky. Again, on another day, the eldest son of a family on the left side of the valley, set out to plow the field. At the same time, a father and son on the right side of the valley also went out to plow the field. Since it was a hot day, the boy plowing on the left side of the valley took off his red *chupa* and placed it on the back of his yak. It was then that the same giant bird appeared and noticed the slightly unusual yak covered in a red cloth. With fear and hesitation, the bird dared not come near the left side of the field; instead, it took the old man and his son, along with their yak, plowing on the right side of the valley. When the boy on the left side of the valley saw the old man and son in the claws of the giant bird, he grabbed his red *chupa,* swung it in the air, and began to scream. The bird immediately released the old man and his son from its clutches. The old man and his son expressed their gratitude to the neighbor and said, "If you had not swung your red *chupa* then we would not be alive today."

It is said that people understood the color red has the strength to ward off evil birds and that is why farmers tie red cloths to their yaks. In time, due to the fondness Tibetans have for ornamentation, they transformed it into the custom of tying prayer flags and other articles of adornment to the yoke of their yaks and red cloths to their yaks' tails.

Other Customs 101

99. Honorific Language
(*bod mir zhe sa mang ba'i skor*)

Tibetans are polite and good-natured people and this is evident not only from their behavior but also from their language. Most languages use honorific terms as a mark of respect for others, but, there are very few languages on this earth with honorific words for each and every action like the Tibetan language. According to the scholarly research on the origin and meaning of honorific words, it is similar to the origin of languages and signs: as the society progressed people gradually started giving more importance to one another and, respect toward elder people. These are all indications of advancement. However, in certain periods, scholars have concluded that honorific language originated from class hierarchy. The reality is, though honorific languages played a special role in hierarchical and class society, it is misleading to assume it originated as a result of hierarchy. In regions where honorific language is widespread, it is customary to speak to an elder with honorific language regardless of their class, birth, or social status.

If a person uses improper honorific words, it is considered disrespectful and the person at fault is thought to be from a rural area. Thus, the use of honorific language is a definite indication of advancement in knowledge.

In some regions of Tibet, there are very few honorific words but they symbolize their respect through the tone of their speech.

—❖—

100. The Tibetan Tradition of Naming
(*bod mi'i ming 'dogs stangs*)

According to the history books of Tibet, a custom of family name (*rus ming*) was not only prevalent in early Tibet, but it was further classified into eighteen different types. The spread of Buddhism in Tibet diminished the importance of *rus ming* and gradually gave way to a new custom of receiving a name from a high lama. High lamas name

102 *A Hundred Customs and Traditions of Tibetan People*

the newborns, conveying either an auspicious or religious meaning. There is also the custom of attaching the parent's surname or the first name for a son or daughter: if Sonam Tsering is the name of the father then his son could be named Sonam Dhondup.

The name of the child may correspond to the day the child was born such as Nyima (Sunday), Dawa (Monday) and Lhakpa (Wednesday). Some Tibetans name their children after an auspicious day in a Tibetan month such as Chonga Tsering, Tsegye Chösum and Namgang. A person ordained as a monk or nun is given a religious name; for example if a person's name is Tashi – after becoming ordained – he is named Lobsang Tashi.

There are many commonly given names in Tibetan and in order to avoid confusion there are different ways of calling out names. Some call out by attaching the family name such as Drongsur Phuntsok and Dekhang Dhondup, while others call out by attaching the regional names like Panam Ngodup and Khangmar Yeshi. There is also a custom of differentiating people into senior, junior and youngster after calling out their names, for example Lhakpa senior, Lhakpa youngster and Lhakpa junior. Furthermore, since there are common names for both genders, Tibetans specify the gender while calling out the names, such as Bhu Tsetan (Boy Tsetan) and Bho-mo Tsetan (Girl Tsetan).

Another important characteristic in the tradition of Tibetan naming is that it relates to the social status and geographical region of one's family. If a name is composed of more than four syllables, such as Lobsang Choekyi Nyima Pel Sangpo, it must be understood as a name of a *tulku*. Jigme Wangchuk, Chogyal Nyima, Thupten Nyima are generally a few names that usually belong to aristocrats, while Nyima, Dawa, Phurbu and Namkhang are names for the common people. Chogpa, Phu Tsering, Phentok and Lhagtsing are some names that suggest one is from the Tsang region. With the mere sound of Yarphel, Wangmo and Dalha, one can understand they are people of the Dokham region.

In order to avoid giving birth to another child, a child is often named Tsamchoe (cut off or to end), Chogpa (sufficient/to be enough) and Chungdak. In the case of parents having only daughters they express their wish for a son by naming the girl Bhuti (bringing a son). In spite of giving birth to many children, many babies die at an early age. If a family has had many infant deaths, in order to maintain long life for a newborn, right after his or her birth the baby is put into a clay pot for a second and named Zakye (literally 'clay born/birth'), Phagkyag (literally 'pig shit') or Khyikyag (literally 'dog shit'). [Although these names are demeaning in other cultures] they act as a symbol in averting harm to the lives of newborn babies.